GREAT TALES
FROM BRITISH HISTORY

THE DOWNFALL OF ANNE BOLEYN

P. FRIEDMANN

D0655013

First published 1884
This edition first published 2015

Amberley Publishing
The Hill, Stroud
Gloucestershire, GL5 4EP

www.amberley-books.com

Copyright © Josephine Wilkinson, 2010, 2013, 2015

The right of Josephine Wilkinson to be identified as the Author of this
work has been asserted in accordance with the Copyrights, Designs
and Patents Act 1988.

All rights reserved. No part of this book may be reprinted or
reproduced or utilised in any form or by any electronic, mechanical
or other means, now known or hereafter invented, including
photocopying and recording, or in any information storage or retrieval
system, without the permission in writing from the Publishers.

British Library Cataloguing in Publication Data.
A catalogue record for this book is available from the British Library.

ISBN 978 1 4456 4466 0 (paperback)
ISBN 978 1 4456 4472 1 (ebook)

Typesetting and Origination by Fakenham Prepress Solutions,
Fakenham, Norfolk NR21 8NN.
Printed in Great Britain.

Introduction

To understand the history of Anne Boleyn's fall, it is absolutely necessary to have a clear and correct idea of the state of England during her lifetime, and of the character of the people she had to deal with. This knowledge, I am sorry to say, cannot be found in any of the numerous works relating to the period of Henry VIII. The writers of these works do not mark with sufficient distinctness the immense difference between England in 1530 and England at the present time; and many of their judgments on Henry VIII and on his contemporaries are superficial and fantastic. I may therefore be allowed as far as possible to attempt to remedy these defects.

Towards the end of the fifteenth century, England was neither like the kingdom of the early Plantagenets, which included nearly a third of France, and ranked among the foremost powers of Europe, nor like the country which under the able rule of Elizabeth developed its internal resources, and profited by the weakness and strife of its neighbours. The country had been ruined by civil wars; its foreign possessions were nearly all gone; the population had been much thinned, had grown unruly, and had lost its habits of industry; the revenue was small, the treasury empty, the administration bad. When Henry VII ascended the throne he set himself to improve the condition of his realm, and in many respects he succeeded. He reorganised the administration, and made it as good and strong as possible. He broke the turbulent spirit of barons and knights, and enforced strict obedience to the royal power. He paid his debts and filled the exchequer, so that his death a very considerable sum was found in the royal coffers. But with all his talent and energy he could not in a few years change a weak and poor country into a strong and prosperous one. Trade and industry could not be called forth at a moment's notice; and without these England, with an indifferent soil and a bad climate, was unable to support a large population, or to amass any great wealth.

Consequently we find that during the first half of the sixteenth century the population of England was about 3.5 million, while that of France was estimated at 14 million, and Charles V could boast of having 16 million subjects in Europe alone. Even in the states of such a prince as Ferdinand of Austria, or the Republic of Venice, contained a larger population than England.

England did not make up by wealth and energy or by other qualities for the smallness of its population. To compare it with the Low Countries or with Upper Italy in regard to trade, industry and wealth, would of course be prosperous; it could not be compared even with France, Germany or Spain. The royal revenue was in proportion to the poverty of the country, totalling about £125,000 a year. The revenue of Charles V was about £1.1 million and that of Francis I, £800,000.

Henry VIII could never occupy that position among Christian princes which was held by Francis I, Charles V or the Pope. But on his accession he found himself with two advantages by which he might have continually augmented his power. The first of these was the geographical position of England, separating France from the northern seas and Spain from the Low Countries. If he had chosen to do so, Henry VIII could have rendered all communication between the French and their friends the Scots most difficult, and could have made it nearly impossible for Spain to trade with the Low Countries or to send soldiers to them. Hence both the French and the Spanish faction desired his alliance, and were always ready to pay a good price even for his neutrality. Henry VII, profiting by this advantage, had exerted considerable influence on the politics of his neighbours, and had obtained all kinds of benefits with very little outlay. While other kings got heavily into debt, Henry VII accumulated large sums of money, which his son on his accession found in the exchequer. This was another great advantage: with ready money armies of foreign mercenaries could be levied, and fleets fitted out, and the bare ability to appear at any moment in the field gave an additional importance to the King of England.

Had Henry VIII been an able and really patriotic king he might with very little trouble to himself and to his subjects have made his country strong and prosperous; after a happy and quiet reign he might have left it one of the foremost powers of Europe. Unhappily for England he was not such a king; the advantages he inherited from his father he wasted; the position he occupied he spoilt as much as it could be spoilt by fickleness and incapacity.

Henry VIII had the ill luck to arrive at the crown at the age of nineteen. His education had been very bad, and quite unfitted for a future king. Of that science by which his father had obtained and consolidated his power Henry VIII learned very little; it was not considered necessary to train him in the methods of administration, finance, politics and war. Additionally, the tyranny of his father had meant that in his teens he had been surrounded by a host of most obedient servants and fulsome flatterers. He had moreover the mischance to marry a woman six years his senior, who was incapable of exercising a wholesome influence on her husband.

His good natural qualities were not, therefore, developed, while his faults and vices were fostered with tender care. He was immensely vain, foolish, weak and thoroughly dishonest. in the correspondence of nearly every ambassador at his court we read of some foolish boast about his riches, his power, and his wisdom, and he put himself on a par with such princes as Charles V or Francis I, princes whose realms were four times as populous as England, whose revenues were even greater in proportion, and who commanded the services of captains and armies such as Henry could never dream of bringing into the field. Henry's acts corresponded with his words. They aimed much more at show and momentary renown than at any real and lasting advantage.

One more fault has been laid to Henry's charge: the coarseness which he always manifested in his relations with the other sex. Even his great panegyrist has been forced to admit the truth of this. Nor can it be excused by the general coarseness of the times. The French under Francis I were perhaps even more dissolute than the English, but Francis was a model of delicacy when compared with Henry. The Spaniards, Italians, and Germans, were all more refined in this respect than the King of England.

If such was the character of King Henry, Catherine of Aragon was altogether different. She was not vain at all, but on the contrary very simple and careless of show, praise or glory. Nor was she weak: she came quickly to a decision, and was most firm in doing what she considered right. She was courageous and did not shrink from responsibility. She was charitable and kind, true and devoted to her friends, and of a forgiving temper towards her enemies. But, on the other hand, Catherine was narrow-minded, violent and wanting in delicacy and tact. She had many individual aims, many single duties, but no comprehensive scheme. Thus she was wholly unfit to strike out a way for herself, especially in the difficult position in which she found herself. She resolved that she would not give way, that no threat or violence should induce her to lay aside her character as the wife of Henry, or to admit her marriage to have been questionable.

That Catherine was quite incapable of flattering Henry, may not be imputed to her as a fault, but it was a disadvantage to her. That she was equally incapable of humouring the whims and caprices of her husband, and of coaxing him into any course she wished him to follow, was a real defect. Instead of leading her husband with 'iron hand in glove of velvet,' she allowed him to feel the whole harshness of her grasp. If she wanted anything, she asked for it directly, without charm of manner; when she was displeased, she too plainly showed her resentment. There was no pliancy in her disposition, and this must have been terribly wounding to the feelings of such a man as Henry. Still, such was his weakness that for nearly four years he accepted her guidance; rather than stand alone he submitted to her disagreeable rule.

That Ferdinand of Aragon cheated his beloved son-in-law more than even Henry would submit to, may have been one of the reasons why in 1513 Catherine suddenly lost the control she had exercised over her husband. Another reason is to be found in the considerable humiliation which the queen in that year inflicted on Henry. The king had in the spring of 1513 crossed the Channel for the purpose of leading the army with which he intended to conquer the whole of France. During his absence the Scots, as hereditary allies of France, had invaded the northern borders, and Catherine, who had been left as regent in England, acted with energy and courage. An army was soon collected of which the Earl of Surrey assumed the command.

But this was not sufficient for the queen; the martial ardour of her forefathers rekindled in her; she took to horse and rode towards the north to place herself at the head of the troops. Surrey's speedy and complete success prevented her from going farther than Woburn, but her vigorous behaviour gained for her the esteem and admiration of the English people. Catherine and Surrey were the heroes of the day, not Henry and his favourites.

And Catherine, with her usual awkwardness, did her best to bring this truth home to Henry. He had sent the Duc de Longuecille, made prisoner at Guinegatte, to England, to be kept there in confinement. Catherine in return sent three Scots over to Henry, with a letter saying that it was no great thing for a man to make another man prisoner, but that here were three men made prisoners by a woman. Henry, jealous of her fame and glory, stung to the quick by her taunt, looked out for a new counsellor.

There was at court one Thomas Wolsey, a priest. He was an able man, and when Henry VIII succeeded, he knew how to flatter the new king: clever, light-hearted, witty and pliant, he amused and pleased his royal master. He had an immense advantage over all his lay competitors for the post of prime minister. Henry could not be jealous of any fame or glory he might gain, for Wolsey was but a priest.

Henry had not, therefore, the slightest hesitation in raising his new favourite to the highest dignities. The bishopric of Tournay and the archbishopric of York were bestowed upon him; the pope was induced to make him a cardinal; and he became lord chancellor. Henry handed over the reins of government to him, trusting his ability and devotion and relying on his quick and firm decision. But Wolsey committed a mistake which was committed by all Henry's ministers: he became rather too forgetful of the feelings of his master. By and by the king began to be annoyed at the way in which the cardinal carried on the whole government of the realm.

During the reign of Wolsey Catherine sank into utter insignificance. Henry's hatred for Ferdinand was, indeed, easily allayed by a splendid present sent to him by the Catholic king with flattering messages, and the anger excited by Catherine did not last long, for when she ceased to rule Henry he found her a very tolerable wife. But one thing told heavily against her: all the sons she bore to the king died shortly after birth; of her children, but one girl, Pricess Mary, survived. To Henry, who ardently longed for a son and heir to succeed him in England and in those realms he always dreamt of conquering, this was a bitter disappointment. When Anne Boleyn began to be a prominent figure at court he had ceased to have any hope of an heir by Catherine, who was then more than forty years of age.

1

Background

By 1526 there had already been a flirtation between Henry and Anne. For some time Anne kept her royal adorer at an even greater distance than the rest of her admirers. She had good reason to do so, for the position which Henry offered her had nothing very tempting to an ambitious and clever girl. When Henry began to pay court to Anne there was already a rumour that he was tired of his queen, that he was greatly annoyed at having no legitimate son to succeed him, and that he might possibly discard Catherine and look out for a younger bride. Anne, who had seen people repudiate their old wives and take new and younger brides, who knew that Henry was on bad terms with the queen and that he ardently wished to have a legitimate son, began to consider what effect all this might have upon her own fortunes. Perceiving that she might be able to displace Catherine, she resolved to spurn every lower prize and to strive with all her might for the crown. From this time she ceased to be merely a clever coquette, and became an important political personage.

If Anne wished to keep her power over Henry unimpaired, to increase her influence and finally to reach the desired end, she had to play a difficult fame. She had to refuse the king's dishonourable proposals, yet had to make her society agreeable to him. Had she yielded, he would very soon have grown tired of her, for she was the most fickle of lovers, having hitherto changed his loves with even greater facility than his good brother of France. But Anne was quite clever enough to succeed; Henry bitterly complained of her severity, but never found her company tiresome. The longer this lasted the more his love for her increased: what had at first been a simple caprice became a violent passion for which he was ready to make great sacrifices.

Anne had come to understand the character of Henry and had learned how he might be ruled. She played her game with such tact that week after week her empire became stronger. Henry allowed himself to be guided by her in matters of state, she succeeded in making him suspicious of Cardinal Wolsey's judgment and intentions, and she encouraged him to act independently behind the back of his prime minister.

The news of Wolsey's death was received by Anne and her friends with an exultation they did not care to conceal. Their great rival was gone, and Anne became daily more overbearing. However, she soon found that the death of Wolsey was not, after all, of much benefit to her. The coalition which had ruined the cardinal having been dissolved, nearly all her allies began to forsake her. The nobles, Suffolk at their head, seeing that she was more arrogant than Wolsey had ever been, were the first to go over to the opposition. Gardiner, who had obtained a promise of the bishopric of Winchester, showed himself less eager to please, and was no longer implicitly trusted. More, Fitzwilliam, the comptroller Guildford and other influential officials were decidedly hostile; and even the Duke of Norfolk was said to have spoken in terms not all favourable to Anne. Her party had for the moment dwindled down to a few of her nearest kinsfolk and personal friends.

In the spring of 1531 her marriage seemed as distant as ever, and the delay did not improve her temper. She appears to have had violent quarrels with Henry, in the course of which she used such strong language that he complained about her to the Duke of Norfolk, saying she did not behave like the queen, who had never in her life used ill words towards him. She did, however, find an ally in Thomas Cromwell, who intended to intimidate England's clergy into granting a divorce.

Anne was created Marchioness of Pembroke in September 1532 with remainder to the heirs male of her body. The words 'lawfully begotten,' which were generally inserted in patents of creation, were significantly left out; any illegitimate son whom Anne might have, would be entitled to the difnity. A thousand pounds in lands were at the same time settled on her, and a few days later she received a present of jewels taken by royal command from the queen. Hitherto Anne, uncertain how long it would take to obtain a divorce, had feared that if she yielded to the king, his passion might cool before she could become his wife. She was cautious, and to provide against the worst, against any unforeseen event that might bear, she asked for a title for herself and any illegitimate son she might bear, and for a grant of lands and jewels.

Henry wished to confirm an alliance between England and France by an interview with Francis I and wished to take Anne with him, partly because he hoped that Francis might be brought to treat her as a person who was shortly to be the Queen of England, whereby a certain sanction would be given to the divorce.

Thomas Cranmer, who had become Archbishop of Canterbury, had sided with the king and Anne on the matter of divorce. In January 1533 Anne had announced to Henry that she was with child. As soon as Cranmer was confirmed as Archbishop by the pope, a bill was submitted to parliament forbidding appeals to Rome, and settling the supreme authority in matrimonial cases on the primate and, in certain cases, on the convocation of the clergy. The divorce was discussed, and although met with opposition, was passed. In April the courtiers were freely discussing the marriage which had taken place on 25 January, and later Anne appeared for the first time in royal state. By 1 June, Anne was crowned queen.

Anne experienced opposition right from the start and Henry himself began to grow lukewarm. He had accomplished his purpose; he had shown the world that, pope and emperor notwithstanding, he had been able to have his own way. Anne, therefore, could no longer play upon his vanity, one of the principal motives by which she had hitherto ruled him. Moreover, he had already become rather tired of her, and thinking that in Anne's condition he was entitled to look out elsewhere for amusement, he began to flirt with the young ladies of the court. She was alarmed by this incipient infidelity, and angrily upbraided him for it; but Henry, who would have been cowed by her indignation a year ago, now brutally replied that she ought to shut her eyes to his pleasures, as others and – he significantly added – her betters had done before her. Anne flew into a violent passion, and

Henry threateningly bid her remember that it was still in his power to lower her as quickly as he had raised her. This made her more furious than ever, and for several days they did not speak to one another.

Anne's chief hope lay in the fact that Henry firmly expected she would give birth to a boy, whom he might proclaim Prince of Wales and appoint his successor. The child was a girl. Henry was exceedingly vexed by what he considered a mischance and a humiliation. And the fact was not only vexatious and wounding to Henry's vanity, it had a real political significance. Englishmen were not accustomed to be ruled by women, and had Anne's child been a boy, some part of the opposition against the king's marriage might have been overcome. Many an Englishman might have abandoned the cause of Mary for that of a Prince of Wales, but between two girls the choice was not difficult: the nation stood by Mary.

2

The Conspiracy

In 1533, after the coronation of Anne, the discontented elements of the nation had been scattered and unorganised; and before they had had time to coalesce, Cromwell's quick hand had carried the principal measures of the government. But at the trial of Lord Dacres, who had been accused of high treason by the king and acquitted, the peers had become aware of their own strength; they had learned that they were nearly all secretly disaffected, and that the crown would not easily obtain from them a verdict against any member of their order. Knowing this, they grew bolder; they opened their minds to one another, and looked about for remedies for the maladies of the time.

The lords having numerous adherents among the gentry, they very easily formed a strong party of resistance. As early as 17 September 1534, Eustache Chapuis received a message from two rich and influential gentlemen, who, afraid of exciting suspicion, would not come to his house, but asked him to meet them as if by chance at an appointed place in the fields. The ambassador went, and they openly told him that they wanted the emperor's help against the tyranny of the king. Several ladies, thinking that their movements were less watched, dared to go to the ambassador's house, and brought Chapuis the same request in their own and in their husbands' names. So strong were the feelings of these fair plotters that one of them, a lady of high rank, forgot all prudence. She threw herself on her knees before Chapuis, and implored him to obtain the emperor's aid. Happily for her, her gentlewomen and the servants of Chapuis stood far off, and although they saw her kneel they could not hear what she said.

A week later a person of very considerable importance appeared on the scene, and communicated with Chapuis. This was Lord

Hussey, who until 1533 had been lord chamberlain to the Princess Mary. He owned very large estates in the midland counties, and had considerable influence at court. He now sent word that before leaving town he wished privately to speak with the French ambassador. To prevent suspicion they had only a short conference, Hussey briefly stating that most of the nobility were extremely dissatisfied with the government, that they had consulted together, and that they wished to be assisted by imperial troops in forcing Henry to dismiss Anne, and to give up the course he was pursuing. For further particulars he referred Chapuis to Lord Darcy, another member of the conspiracy.

The ambassador, eager to know the whole business, sent on the following day a confidential agent to Darcy, who immediately disclosed their designs at greater length. In the northern counties alone, he said, there were already sixteen earls and barons, who in this matter were all of the same opinion. If the emperor sent men of war and a few troops to the mouth of the Thames, and if a band of good hackbutters, some experienced officers and a supply of arms and ammunition were landed in the north, the lords would rise against the king. They would unfurl the imperial standard, adding a crucifix to it. Their forces were already considerable – Darcy himself undertook to raise 8,000 men – and many others would certainly join them. Of his associates Darcy named but two, the Earl of Derby and Lord Dacres of Greystock, the peer who had just been acquitted of a charge of high treason. Of possible opponents in the north, Darcy knew of none except the Earl of Northumberland; and he might be easily arrested, as he had no following, and his own servants would not support him. Charles was advised to befriend James V of Scotland, who secretly aspired to the hand of his cousin, Princess Mary; and the intention of the conspirators seems to have been to proclaim James and Mary under the auspices of the emperor as feudal overlord. According to Darcy, they had no doubt of success.

The communication was so important, the details given by Darcy seemed so likely to be accurate, that Chapuis wrote at once to the emperor to ask for instructions. He did not venture to offer an opinion directly, but he clearly showed that he thought the plan feasible; and he was persuaded that if it could be carried out it would be of the greatest advantage.

Charles received the ambassador's letter just after the Count of Nassau had been despatched to the French court. From a simply political point of view, the offer was tempting enough, since it might enable the emperor to obtain a firm footing in England, and secure for him a strong alliance against France. It had also a most seductive aspect for Charles's fancy. He was the last emperor who seriously thought of regaining the power that had been wielded by Charles the Great. He dreamt of being recognised as the supreme lord of the western world, of establishing that monarchy which Dante had praised, which was to heal all wounds and strife, and to extend the rule of Christendom over the whole earth. Two kingdoms had been foremost among those which had refused to submit to the authority of the Kaiser – France and England. Long ago an English king had been obliged to take an oath of fealty to the emperor, but Richard I had forgotten his promises as soon as he had recovered his liberty, and they had been wholly disregarded by his successors. For more than three centuries no emperor had pretended to exercise power in England, and only a few forms remained to remind the curious and the learned of the ancient tie.

But now the English nobles, writhing under the tyranny of Henry, appealed to the emperor. Admitting their dependence upon him, they wished to legalise their rising by fealty to the higher lord, and offered to unfurl his standard. The English leopards were to be superseded by the Roman eagle, the imperial power in England was to become a reality. It was a splendid prospect, and the resolution to turn from it must have cost Charles V a bitter pang. But dreamer as the emperor was, he was also a keen and farsighted politician. For the present, with Soliman, Barbarossa and Francis I threatening him, he could not wish for a rising which might prove the signal for general war. He wanted to fight Barbarossa separately, and for that purpose it was necessary to have peace with France, which rebellion in England would render impossible. So the English were to wait until Tunis was taken.

Chapuis was ordered to give general assurances of good will, and to remain in communication with Hussey, Darcy, and their confederates, but not to go any further. He was directed, too, to obtain information about Reginald Pole, regarding whom the emperor had lately received a report from Venice, describing him as a person of some importance. With this part of his instructions Chapuis easily complied. Reginald was closely related to Lord Abergavenny, the ambassador's old friend, to the Earl of Westmoreland, and to Lord Latimer; and his mother,

Countess of Salisbury in her own right, had been the governess of the princess and was universally respected and admired. Lord Montague, the elder brother of Reginald, and Sir Geoffrey Pole, his younger brother, had already communicated with Chapuis, and were ready to fight for Mary; and Chapuis thought that if a rising took place, and if imperial troops were sent to support it, his presence would add considerably to the popularity of the insurrection.

Chapuis received his instructions at a moment when it seemed as if no rising would be necessary to drive Anne from power; for during the few weeks which had elapsed between the despatch of his letter and the arrival of Charles's reply, the conservative party had gained an important ally. In the spring of 1534 Henry had already shown signs of being weary of the woman he now called his wife. Eighteen months of possession were a long time for so fickle a lover, and he had begun to pay marked attention to a young and very handsome lady at court. Who she was I have not been able to discover; neither Chapuis nor the French ambassador mention her name in the despatches which have been preserved. The only thing certain is, that she was not Anne's later rival, Jane Seymour.

Henry's affection for Anne had seemed to revive when she had led him to believe that there was again a chance of his having a male heir; but when she was obliged to confess that she had been mistaken he returned to the young lady, and paid court to her in a more public manner than ever. Anne became very angry, and in her bold and overbearing way tried to send her rival away from court. But she presumed too much on Henry's weakness, overlooking the fact that she had no authority except what she derived from the influence she exerted over him. As soon as he heard of her attempt to interfere with his amours, he sent her a most insulting message, informing her that she had good reason to be content with what he had done for her, because if it were still to be done he would not do it. Let her, he said, remember where she had come from, and not be overbearing.

The new favourite proved to be a strong adherent of Catherine; and she went so far as to send a message to Mary to be of good cheer, for things might change very soon. Whenever she could, she would do her best to serve the princess.

In proportion as the power of the lady increased, that of Anne decreased; and the courtiers, ever ready to abandon a falling favourite,

were eager to desert Anne, whom most of them hated. They s̤
an opportunity of showing how little they really cared for hᵤ
October Mary and little Elizabeth were taken to Richmond from ʉ
More, where they had been spending the autumn, and where Mary
had been visited by the gentry of the neighbourhood. When they
were at Richmond, Anne, attended by many ladies and gentlemen,
went to see her daughter. No sooner had she gone in to Elizabeth
than the whole throng of courtiers, the Dukes of Norfolk and Suffolk
at their head, went to pay their respects to Mary. It was impossible for
Anne to console herself even by an outburst of anger at the honour
shown to her enemy; she had meekly to submit to what she could not
but consider a deliberate affront.

Of course the Boleyn faction tried every means to avert the dangers
by which they were confronted. Lady Rochford, Anne's sister-in-law,
began to intrigue against the favourite, hoping indirectly to shake her
credit and to oblige her to leave court. But the plot was detected, and
the king in his rage inflicted on her the fate she had tried to prepare
for Anne's rival; so that Anne was now deprived of the company both
of her sister and of her sister-in-law. Occasionally she attempted to
hold her ground, and once she complained of the insolence with
which the favourite treated her, but Henry turned his back on her and
went away. Her family shared her disgrace. Sir Francis Brian having
brought an action against Lord Rochford, the influence of Henry was
exerted in favour of Brian.

The moment seemed favourable for an attempt to re-establish good
relations between Henry and the Holy See. In September Clement
VII had fallen dangerously ill, and the king had ordered Gregorio da
Casale to repair at once to Rome to watch events, and, if possible, to
induce the pope on his deathbed to recall his sentence. The French
ambassador, who had been asked to use his influence for the same
purpose, had hesitated to do so, but Casale had nevertheless remained
at Rome working for his patron. Shortly afterwards Clement died,
and Cardinal Farnese, formerly accounted a staunch friend of King
Henry, was chosen in his place. Paul III – so the new pope decided to
call himself – adopted a moderate tone, and showed himself anxious
for a reconciliation. He spoke with the Cardinal of Lorraine, the
most important of the French members of the sacred college, and the
cardinal promised to go himself to England to bring the king back to

me. Casale wrote in a very hopeful manner, and
ty in England strained every nerve to profit by

nown at the French court, and Francis and his
ake advantage of it. Although they had refused
made by Charles V for a marriage between Mary and the
Duke of Angoulême, they had not broken off the negotiation. What
they really desired was a marriage between Mary and the dauphin. If
this could be brought about, Anne would be easily disposed of, for
Henry would either fall with her, or he would have to give her up. In
the latter case he would have to take back Catherine, from whom no
further issue was to be expected. England would then, after the death
of Francis, be united to France; and the new kingdom, commanding
both sides of the Channel, would be the foremost power in Europe.
Such were the hopes entertained by the French government; but it
was not to be supposed that Charles would readily assent to a scheme
that might be so perilous for the empire. The French saw that only
by clever intrigue could they hope to persuade him to sanction the
substitution of the dauphin for Angoulême.

The first thing they had to do was to keep up the distrust between
Henry and Charles, and to obtain as much as possible from Henry's
fears. About the end of October Philippe de Chabot, admiral of
France, was sent on a special mission to England, and although
his instructions do not seem to have survived, sufficient evidence
remains as to his charge. He was to tell Henry that Charles had
proposed through the Count of Nassau two marriages, one between
his son Philip and the youngest daughter of Francis – which was true
– the other between the dauphin and Mary – which was not true.
Moreover, he was to say that Charles had offered Francis the duchy
of Milan after the death of the reigning duke, and in the meantime
a pension of 100,000 crowns. This also was untrue, for the offer was
to hold good only if the duke should die childless, and the sum was
much smaller. After this Chabot was to assure Henry that Francis
intended to remain faithful to him, and to reject Charles's proposals.
But Henry was to be asked to forego the title of King of France, and
to accept in exchange a very chimerical title to certain estates in
the Low Countries which were to be taken by Henry himself from
Charles. Francis desired to be relieved of the obligation to pay the

pensions due on account of the treaty of Amiens, and Chabot was to beg Henry to reconsider his policy towards Rome, and either to submit to the pope at once or to reopen the negotiations so suddenly broken off in the spring.

These instructions were very cleverly drawn, for, by a treaty signed in 1518, Mary and the dauphin had actually been betrothed, and Chabot was to base his negotiations on this treaty. If Henry repudiated it, he would set the dauphin free to marry the Infanta Doña Juana, a match which of course would strengthen the Spanish influence in France and draw Francis away from England. If, on the contrary, to prevent the match with the infanta, Henry admitted that the betrothal was still valid, the game of Francis would be half won. It was a disagreeable dilemma for the King of England, and still more disagreeable for the Boleyns.

Chabot left the French court on 20 October, and having a very numerous train, he travelled slowly. On 8 November he arrived at Calais, and on the 11th he crossed to Dover. Here he waited for his servants and horses, so that his entry into London was delayed until the 20th. The admiral found a state of things very different from that which he had expected. The conservative party seemed to have no influence whatever; and the English government, instead of showing any desire for a reconciliation with Rome, was quietly pursuing the opposite course.

Henry and his advisers were certainly not ignorant of the state of public feeling and of the conspiracy which was being formed, for Cromwell's spies must have warned him of what was going on. But the government was not in a position to take proceedings against the conspirators. It might have secured from a packed jury the conviction of some of the lesser malcontents; but it could not venture to attack the leaders of the movement. An attempt to bring any of the lords to trial would almost certainly have failed, and failure in a matter of so much importance would have seriously damaged the authority of the crown. Fortunately for ministers, they knew that the conspirators now hoped to gain their object by some less dangerous method than open rebellion. Moreover, the winter was setting in, a most unpropitious time for an insurrection. English peasants could not lie out in cold and damp, and if a force were raised against Henry, however powerful it might seem to be, it would dwindle away before the inclemency of the season.

The government made use of the respite to strengthen itself for the coming struggle. Henry had indeed, no choice but to go forward with the task he had begun. If he retreated now, he would encourage the opposition, and lose, perhaps, not only all that accession to the prerogative which he had gained during the last few years, but a great part of the authority which had long been obnoxious to peers and commoners alike. He would have to sacrifice his trustiest and ablest ministers, and to substitute for them at the council board the very men who resisted his pretensions. He would become so weak a king, while the peers would become so elated and so popular, that the olden times of York and Lancaster might be revived, and in the midst of the turmoil the Tudor king might disappear. It was, therefore, absolutely necessary to complete the measures which had been taken for the assertion of the royal supremacy.

Parliament met on 4 November, and ministers introduced a number of bills which clearly showed that neither the growing dislike of Henry for Anne, nor his fancy for her rival, had altered his policy. First of all came the famous Act of Supremacy, by which the king was to be declared the only supreme head on earth of the Church of England. This bill was easily carried: a fortnight after the opening of the session, two days before Chabot arrived in London, it had already passed.

The admiral, being convinced that the Act of Supremacy was due to Anne's influence, took pains to indicate that the feelings of his master towards her had greatly changed. For two days after he had been received by Henry he did not even mention her name, so that at last the king asked whether he would not go and see the queen. 'As it pleases your highness,' was the cold answer. He had no message for her; and he showed that he would wait upon her only out of courtesy to the king. While Chabot strongly marked his indifference to Anne, he begged for permission to see the Princess Mary. His application was refused, but he found means to let it be generally known that the request had been made. And when his gentlemen and servants were asked whether a marriage had been arranged between the dauphin and the infanta, they asserted that no such plan was thought of. How could it be? Was not the dauphin betrothed to the princess?

At the same time both Chabot and the resident French ambassador, Morette, were ostentatiously polite to Chapuis; and in the same spirit

Chapuis responded to their advances. There was a show of cordiality between the two embassies which boded no good to Henry and Anne.

On hearing from Chabot what his instructions were, Henry tried a counter move. He could not see why the dauphin should marry Mary, who was illegitimate; but might not Angoulême marry Elizabeth? Chabot did not absolutely reject the proposal, as it would not necessarily prevent the other match, and Henry might be persuaded to give a considerable dowry. But the French representative was careful to leave the impression that he was not satisfied.

An incident which occurred on the evening before Chabot's departure from England well depicts Anne's position. On 1 December there was a ball at court, and the admiral sat with Henry and Anne on a raised platform looking at the dances. Palamede Gontier, treasurer of Brittany and chief secretary to the embassy, being in the hall, Henry wished to present him to Anne, and went to fetch him. Anne kept her eyes on the king as he made his way through the crowd, and saw that he stopped before reaching Gontier, and forgot everything in the conversation of a young lady – her rival. By constant tension of mind, Anne's health had been very much impaired; and she burst into a fit of hysterical laughter which lasted for several minutes. The admiral, indignant at her behaviour, angrily asked whether she laughed at him; and although Anne, on regaining her composure, tried to explain, she could not allay his resentment. Chabot reported the incident with remarks by no means flattering to Anne.

Next day, while Chabot was standing in the hall of his house, Sir William Fitzwilliam, Sir Nicholas Carew, Cromwell and other ministers of Henry came to pay their respects to him. He received them with marked coldness, but when Chapuis was announced Chabot went to meet him, greeted him most amiably, and, leaving the Englishmen to themselves, drew the imperial ambassador aside to assure him of his goodwill and to complain of Henry. These demonstrations were intended as much for the English as for Chapuis, the admiral wishing it to be clearly understood that he was decidedly displeased with the king and with Anne.

Chabot had really some reason to complain of Henry's behaviour. Even while he was in England a bill was brought in by the government to enforce obedience to the Act of Supremacy. By this bill it was to be made high treason to deny to the king and queen or their heirs the dignity, style and name of their royal estate, or to call them heretic, schismatic, or infidel. The measure met with considerable opposition; and after long and animated debates in both houses it was passed only when the government accepted two amendments intended to mitigate its severity. The first of these was that the Act should not take effect until 1 February following, when it would be generally known, and nobody would be likely to incur its penalties unawares. The second amendment seemed even more important, for it decreed that only malicious denial of the king's title should be considered high treason. This clause was introduced for the purpose of shielding persons who, like Fisher and More, would offer no opinion on the question.

Fisher and More had now been prisoners for many months. The severity with which they had at first been treated had soon been relaxed; they had been allowed to obtain books and writing materials, to see their friends, and to enjoy the liberties of the Tower – that is, to take a walk either in the inner garden or on the leads behind the battlements. But after the passing of the Act of Supremacy they were asked by the council, which went to the Tower for the purpose, to accept the new law. Both desired to be excused; whereupon, to punish them for their obstinacy, the privileges they had enjoyed were withdrawn. Their books and writing materials were taken from them, and they could correspond only by stealth.

Had the bill creating new kinds of treason passed in its original form, the two prisoners might have suffered immediately. As it was, the rigour of their confinement was not to last very long, and for a moment they were to have a chance of regaining their freedom. The last month of 1534 was particularly disagreeable to Henry. Chabot, as already said, had plainly shown that he was no longer the friend he had been; and, as he had hitherto been very favourable to Henry and Anne, this was an ominous sign. Nor was it much more encouraging that although couriers came from France none of them brought an answer to the proposals made to the French admiral. Chabot had, indeed, travelled home rather slowly, but even this could not account for the delay. Henry was also troubled by tidings which reached him from Spain. A considerable body of troops was being raised in that country, ships were being got ready, and an important expedition was clearly about to be undertaken. As the King of England was not aware of the real object of these preparations, he became somewhat suspicious. There were ships enough in the Biscayan harbour to bring over the whole force to the English shores, and he had no fleet to intercept them, nor an army to withstand the troops if they landed.

In these circumstances Henry thought it expedient to conciliate his enemies both abroad and at home. Although most rigorous measures had been passed, the government began to act warily, and the first to feel the good effect of the change were the prisoners in the Tower. Their confinement was once more made less strict; they were allowed to write and receive letters, and to see their friends. If a letter of Palamede Gontier, printed by Lelaboureur, may be considered good evidence, Fisher was even permitted to leave the Tower on bail, and to repair to the court at Westminster. In any case, from the end of December to the middle of February, they were treated with comparative favour. And so were Catherine and Mary, who during this period were not molested by messages from the council.

At the same time it was thought that some arrangement might be come to with Charles V; and in Paris, towards the end of December, Sir John Wallop tried to open negotiations with Viscount Hanart, the imperial ambassador at the French court. Hanart did not pay much attention to these overtures, but neither did he refuse to listen to them. A few weeks later, on 20 January, Wallop returned to the subject. He called on Hanart, and stated that he had consulted some of his friends in England, and that in their opinion a compromise might be arrived at on the following basis. Let the emperor promise not to proceed in the matter of the divorce by violence as long as Henry lived; and in the meantime the queen would be treated well, and otherwise matters would remain in suspense. Hanart was very reserved, but he wrote an account of the conversation to Granvelle and asked for instructions.

The time seemed in every way propitious for a reconciliation. The credit of the Boleyns was daily decreasing, their enemies were becoming more aggressive, and persons belonging to the class who like to be on the winning side were forsaking Anne and her relatives. She knew this, and was in great anguish of mind. She could not conceal from herself that the ally on whom she had most firmly reckoned, Francis I, was disposed to desert her cause; and she clearly understood that without his help the emperor could not be resisted. If Francis formed an alliance with Charles against England, Henry might save himself by speedy submission, but Anne would have to be sacrificed.

Happily for her, the antagonism between Charles and Francis was so deep-rooted that a real alliance was impossible. After Chabot's return Francis had hesitated, for the offers made by the emperor seemed very tempting. But the French king was well aware that the expedition which was to be undertaken against Khairredin was meant to deprive him of an ally; and he suspected that Charles's proposals were intended to amuse him and to keep him quiet while Tunis was being conquered. While he was balancing between two courses open to him, he received news which filled him with indignation against the emperor. A rumour had gone abroad in Germany that Francis had agreed to abandon the German Lutheran princes; and the French, rightly or wrongly, traced the report to an imperial source. If it were not contradicted he would lose the friendship of his German allies, and would not be able, as heretofore, to levy landsknechts to fight his battles. On 18 January Francis saw Viscount Hanart, to whom he violently complained of what he had heard. The viscount tried in vain to explain the thing away: he could not appease the king's anger or lull his suspicions. Incensed against the emperor, Francis bethought himself once more of the English alliance. An answer to Henry's proposals was made out, and three days after Hanart's audience Palamede Gontier took it to the English court.

But even now the long expected message was by no means what Anne would have liked. The conditions of Francis were rather hard. No wonder, then, that she looked haggard and worn, and that when, two days after his arrival, Gontier saw her at a ball at court and gave her a letter from Chabot, she betrayed her anxiety. She complained that by coming so late he had made the king very suspicious. It was necessary, she said, that Chabot should put matters right, for she found herself in even greater difficulties than before her marriage. She entreated Gontier to pray the admiral in her name to look after her affairs, of which she could not, unhappily, inform him at such length as she wished, because of the prying eyes of the king and the courtiers. She added that she would not be able to write, nor would she have an opportunity of seeing him again, and even now she dared not remain with him any longer. And so she left him, and the treasurer followed Henry into the ball-room wondering what all this meant. 'I assure you, my lord,' he wrote to Chabot, 'by what I can make out she is not at her ease.'

Immediately after his arrival, Gontier had been called to court, and had had a long audience of the king. First of all the marriage of Elizabeth with the Duke of Angoulême, which Henry had proposed, was spoken of. It would be necessary, Palamede Gontier said, that Elizabeth should be made perfectly sure of her rank, as the Duke of Angoulême could not marry a woman whose social and political status was a matter of doubt. Henry angrily protested that Elizabeth was the undoubted heir to the crown, and generally recognised as such; but if any doubt remained in the mind of Francis, he might easily set it at rest by obliging the pope to recall the sentence given by Clement, and to declare the marriage with Catherine to have been null and void from the beginning. Henry was most anxious that this should be done, for reasons which Gontier perhaps guessed, and which ought to have made the French reluctant to commit themselves any further in the matter.

Gontier went on to state what portion Francis would expect the little girl to bring to him and to his son. It was nothing less than the renunciation by Henry of the title of King of France, and the extinction of all pensions, arrears, or payments which the French were by treaties bound to make to him – a sum of about 120,000 crowns a year. At this exorbitant claim Henry's anger broke forth, and he could not for some time regain his equanimity. In the end he said that 50,000 crowns of perpetual pension he was ready to give up, but the 60,000 which were to be paid to him personally during life he would not relinquish. No decision was arrived at, and as it had grown late the conference was postponed to the following day.

Early next morning Palamede Gontier went to Cromwell's house at Austin friars. The French had hitherto shown little attention to the secretary, having failed to realise the full extent of his power. They now tried to make up for past neglect. Gontier brought complimentary messages from the king and from the admiral, and threw out broad hints that Cromwell would profit by supporting the demands of France. The secretary listened politely, and professed goodwill towards Francis; but he made no positive promise or answer. Although Gontier flattered himself that he had made some impression on him, Cromwell remained at heart as anti-French as he had ever been.

From Austin friars the treasurer took his way to Westminster, where he met the Dukes of Norfolk and Suffolk, both of whom showed themselves most friendly. Gontier remained at court until after dinner, when he was called into the royal presence. Henry was still angry at the extravagant claims of Francis, and complained of the negotiations which had been kept up with the emperor. The following day was Candlemas, and Gontier went to the royal chapel. After the service Henry invited him into his closet, and in a more pacified tone began to talk about the proposed meeting between himself and the French king. He was much gratified to hear that the Queen of Navarre and the daughters of Francis were to come to the interview. This flattered his vanity, and put him in better humour. The audience ended with a significant request from the French king. Lord Rochford and Sir Nicholas Carew were rival candidates for the next vacant garter, and Francis asked that it might be bestowed on Carew. Henry promised to remember his good brother's wishes.

That same evening – the evening of the ball at which Gontier met poor Anne – the royal council drew up the official answer to the French proposals. It was even less favourable than the reply given by the king. The perpetual pension he had declared himself willing to resign, the council would not part with. As to the marriage, they proposed that commissioners should be sent at Whitsuntide to Calais, there to debate the conditions. Should the admiral be one of them, the Duke of Norfolk, Sir William Fitzwilliam and Cromwell would go to meet him. Neither the father nor the brother of Anne were to take part in the negotiations which would settle the future fate of her daughter – another certain sign of their disgrace. The time of the conference was intentionally fixed at a distant date, that Francis might try to obtain from Paul III a reversal of the sentence given by Pope Clement.

The English opponents of Henry's policy were now in high spirits. On the day after the ball at court, Morette gave a great dinner party, at which the Dukes of Norfolk and Suffolk, Sir William Weston, prior of St John, Lord Abergavenny, and other influential adherents of the papacy were present. Palamede Gontier told them of the *auto da fé* at Paris lately, when Francis himself with his sons had marched in the procession and had watched the torturing and burning of a good number of Protestants. The English lords were delighted to hear of this, and praised Francis for what he had done. There could be no doubt, Gontier wrote to Chabot, as to what they themselves would like to do in England.

Henry was at this time in a state of great perplexity. Annoyed by Anne's jealousy, and angry with her for not having borne him the son and heir he had expected, he was anxious to be rid of her; and the most natural way of accomplishing his purpose seemed to be a second divorce. Cranmer, he felt sure, would make no difficulties, but would declare the second marriage, like the first, to be null and void. Having thought the matter over, he opened his mind to some of his most trusted counsellors. Who they were does not appear; but their answer averted the blow which he thought of striking at Anne. If the king, they replied, wished to repudiate Anne, he must restore the rights of Catherine, and acknowledge Mary as his heir and successor. Henry had hoped that the marriage with Catherine might still be dissolved by the pope, and that he would then be delivered from all difficulty. He had overlooked the fact that even if Paul III revoked his predecessor's sentence it would be extremely dangerous to discard Anne after all that had been done in her favour. The Catholics would be as hostile as before, and he would excite the enmity of the Protestants, who would decline to believe in new scruples of conscience. As his advisers urged, therefore, it was necessary for him to make up his mind whether he would have Catherine or Anne for wife; the choice lay with him, but was limited to these two. This was at last made apparent to Henry, and on his decision the fate of Anne depended.

3

Fisher & More

Anne and her friends were in serious peril, and she might have succumbed at once had she not regained the help of Cromwell. The secretary had not been much impressed by Gontier's fair words; he was still hostile to France, and saw with apprehension the growing power of the aristocratic party and of his bitter enemy the Duke of Norfolk. Having identified himself so closely with the measures against the Roman Church, he could not but fear that, if its authority were re-established, he would fare very badly at its hands. In order to prevent the possibility of a reaction, he resolved to support Anne; and perhaps it was he who explained to Henry the danger of a second divorce.

The troubles of the Boleyns had been due in a great measure to the influence of the new favourite, whose reign had now lasted nearly six months – for Henry, rather a long time. It occurred to them that their prospects might be improved if the king were under the dominion of a more friendly beauty; and in the hope that he might be fascinated they brought to court Anne's pretty cousin, Margaret Shelton, daughter of the governess of Mary. The scheme may not have been very dignified, but it was eminently successful. On 25 February, little more than three weeks after the ball at which Gontier had seen Anne in despair, Eustache Chapuis wrote: 'The lady who formerly enjoyed the favour of this king does so no longer; she has been succeeded in her office by a first cousin of the concubine, daughter of the new governess of the princess'.

The defeat of the imperialist favourite led to renewed agitation among the malcontents, for with the advent of Margaret Shelton disappeared the last hope that by means of female influence a reversal of policy might be obtained. Even during the preceding winter, when it had been found that the fair partisan of Catherine and Mary was not able to make Henry altogether obedient to her will, the members of the opposition had drawn together again, and numerous recruits had swollen their ranks. In the end of December 1534, the only peer north of the Trent who had been favourable to Anne, the Earl of Northumberland, professed to be deeply offended by the insolence of the Boleyns, and to be ready to join the confederacy against his former love. This was reported to Chapuis by the earl's physician. The conspirators were rather suspicious of Northumberland, whom they knew to be wayward and fickle, and they warned Chapuis to be very careful in dealing with him; but if Anne's enemies were unable to consider him a trustworthy ally, it was at least certain that she could not regard even him as a faithful friend.

More important men now began to communicate with Chapuis. Lord Sandys, the chamberlain of the household, who had retired from court on the plea of sickness, sent a message to the ambassador by his physician to the effect that it would be easy for Charles V to conquer England, and that he himself would willingly rise if the emperor would undertake to support an insurrection. A few weeks later, the Marquis of Exeter protested that he was prepared to shed his heart's blood in the cause of Catherine; and Lord Bray, a wealthy peer who was highly esteemed for his learning and energy, applied to Chapuis for the text of a prophecy that there would be a revolt against the government, and begged for a cipher by means of which some malcontent lords might safely correspond with one another. He also wished to be permitted to speak with Chapuis about these matters. The latter request the ambassador did not think fit to comply with, as it might awaken suspicion, but otherwise he returned a friendly and encouraging answer, asking only that his correspondent would wait for a more convenient season.

In February Mary had fallen seriously ill. After some time the king allowed the queen's physician to attend her, and sent his own physician, Dr Butts, to consult with him. The two doctors did not limit their conversation to medical matters, but very soon began to talk of politics. Dr Butts made no mystery of his opinions. He said that the life of the queen and the princess might be spared if the king fell ill, since he would then listen to reason and understand his errors, but that otherwise they could be saved only by the employment of force. It was well for the king, he added, that the emperor did not know with how little trouble he might make himself master of England.

The aim of the conspirators being to proclaim Mary, Chapuis feared that if the signal for revolt were given she would be put to death; and he had sounded her whether she would be ready to save herself by flight. Finding that she was willing to do whatever might seem to him to be expedient, he decided that if he received the emperor's permission, and if Mary remained at Greenwich, she should be carried off and put on board a light rowing vessel which would carry her to Flanders; but in consequence of her illness this plan had to be abandoned. It happened about this time that several of Anne's adversaries, among them her uncle, Sir Edward Boleyn, were dining with Chapuis; and with them he made an appointment to go on the Saturday following to Lord Darcy, with whom he was anxious to confer about measures for the princess's safety. Much to the disappointment of Chapuis, this engagement could not be fulfilled; and, knowing the watchfulness of Cromwell's spies, he did not venture to go alone. He despatched a confidential agent, however, and to this messenger Darcy said that if civil war were proclaimed he believed Henry would send Catherine and Mary to the Tower, and keep them there as hostages for his own security. Now, Sir William Kingston, captain of the king's guard and constable of the Tower, had entered into correspondence with the conspirators, and had declared himself a devoted adherent of the two ladies. If they were entrusted to him, they would be in no danger whatever. This intelligence, which was confirmed from other quarters, somewhat reassured the ambassador; but as a thoroughgoing adherent of the king might be put in Sir William Kingston's place, Chapuis was still of opinion that Mary ought to be removed from England. In April she was taken to Eltham, and he hoped that it might be possible to have her conveyed from that place to the river below Gravesend. If men were sent in pursuit, they would probably wish her good speed and take care not to overtake her. The chief difficulty would be to get her out of the house, which was strongly guarded by a body of royal servants under the command of Sir John Shelton.

The government, knowing much of what was going on, caused the chief conspirators to be closely watched, and when some of them applied for permission to leave the court it was not granted. Cromwell wished to keep them near, so that they might always be surrounded by spies.

While Anne and her party – thanks to Margaret Shelton – seemed to be recovering their power, they were threatened by a new danger. Early in March, Cromwell caught a severe cold, and was obliged to keep his room for a few days. Impatient at the confinement and wishing to speak with Chapuis, he went out too soon, had a relapse to which he did not pay sufficient attention, and on Monday the 22nd, broke down altogether. He seems to have suffered from inflammation of the lungs. For a fortnight his life was in danger, and for nearly three weeks he could not transact any business. During this time his enemies, the friends of Catherine and Mary, tried to exercise some influence on Henry, and he seemed not unwilling to hear them; but Cromwell recovered, and at once destroyed their hopes. Whoever had dared to speak in favour of the queen and the princess was soundly rated and threatened by the secretary.

Before Cromwell's illness, it had been determined that the form of oath which had been prepared towards the close of the session, and to which the clergy attending convocation had been compelled to subscribe, should be imposed upon all who were suspected of hostility to the new measures. Now another step in the same direction was taken; a proclamation was issued against those who still adhered to the pope, or who used his name or style in the service of the Church. Strict inquiry was to be made, and offenders were to be severely punished. The secular clergy in general offered little opposition, but there were monks who showed themselves less yielding. The priors of the Carthusian monasteries, men renowned for their ascetic virtue and piety, assembled at the Charterhouse, near London, and protested against the new edict. Cromwell summoned them before him, and as they boldly proclaimed their intention to disobey what they considered an unjust command they were committed to the Tower to await judgment. They were not kept long in suspense. On 29 April they were arraigned at the Guildhall, found guilty, and condemned to the usual punishment of traitors. No mercy was shown to them; on 4 May the three priors and a Brigitin monk from Syon were hanged, cut down alive, disembowelled, beheaded and quartered. The Duke of Richmond, Henry's bastard son, the

Duke of Norfolk, Wiltshire, Rochford, Norris, and other courtiers went to Tyburn to witness their death.

By this time the negotiations about the proposed meeting at Calais had been nearly brought to an end. On 5 March, after a stay of five weeks, Gontier had left England to give Francis an account of his mission. On the 25th he came over once more, remaining about a week in England. He took back flattering and promising messages from Henry, to which the admiral of France answered in the same strain. The 23 May was fixed as the day on which the commissioners were to assemble, and Henry looked forward with confidence to the result.

Cromwell was less sanguine, for he knew from the beginning what would be the effect of the execution of men so highly respected as the Carthusian monks. The English Observants, Carthusians and Brigitins were not simply English subjects, they were members of international religious societies which everywhere commanded respect and sympathy. Henry had persecuted those monastic orders which were esteemed by Catholic and Protestant alike, while he favoured the members of confraternities notorious for their sloth, their ignorance, and their immorality. Preachers on the Continent vehemently denounced the cruelty of a king who had caused men like Haughton to be executed, and men like Peyto to be banished. In France the feeling against Henry seems to have become intensely bitter, and the English alliance was most unpopular.

Being certain that in these circumstances the commissioners at Calais would be unable to agree, Cromwell resolved to have nothing to do with their proceedings. He pretended that he was not yet well enough to go, and, as the Boleyns had been restored to favour, Lord Rochford was named in his stead. On 19 and 20 May the English commissioners arrived at Calais, and on the 22nd they were joined by Chabot, with whom were Genoulhiac, master of the horse; Poyet, president of the parliament of Paris; and Bochetel, secretary for finance. What Cromwell had foreseen came to pass. The French would not depart from the conditions proposed through Palamede Gontier, and they are said to have added a clause to the effect that if for any reason, after the conclusion of the treaty, Henry broke off the match, he would forfeit all pensions and arrears due to him by the King of France. On all the points in dispute the admiral was immovable, so that after two sittings Norfolk perceived that no understanding such as Henry desired could be arrived at.

Lord Rochford crossed to Dover, and galloped straight to the court to give an account of the French demands. On his arrival he went at once to his sister, who could scarcely bring herself to believe the news he reported. On the following days she relieved her feelings by saying all the ill she could of Francis and of the French people; and it was observed that whereas Morette had hitherto been invited to all her parties, he was henceforth conspicuously absent.

When he had seen the king, Rochford left for Calais with the same haste with which he had come, taking with him supplementary instructions to Norfolk. They were to prove fruitless. Francis, in consenting to treat with Henry regarding the marriage of Angoulême and Elizabeth, wanted to obtain such a dowry, in ready money, subsidies, or renunciation of pensions, as would make it worth his while to sanction the match without taking into account any hopes the little girl might have of succeeding to the English throne. He wished, too, to refrain from doing anything that would imperil the treaty by which a marriage between the dauphin and the Princess Mary had been arranged. And he not only objected to join Henry in his revolt against the Holy See, but strongly advised that by some kind of submission the English schism should be brought to an end. Henry, on the other hand, desired by the proposed marriage to make sure of the French alliance, and he would not accept any conditions which would render it equally advantageous to Francis to side with Mary and her adherents. He was not inclined to give a large dowry, for his vanity revolted against the idea that his, the great King Henry's, daughter was not by herself a brilliant match for a younger son of the French king. He insisted that Angoulême should be sent over to him, with some idea perhaps that he would then have a hostage for the good behaviour of Francis. And he advanced preposterous claims as to the position the young duke was to occupy in France, should he by right of his wife succeed to the English crown.

The English commissioners in vain strove to overcome the resistance of Chabot and his colleagues. The French no longer stood in urgent need of the English alliance, since it was open to them, if they pleased, by accepting the overtures of Nassau, to come to terms with the emperor. It was Henry who was now in danger of finding himself confronted by a hostile coalition; it was he, the French thought, who ought to be ready to make sacrifices. But this he declined to do, and his commissioners succeeded only in irritating Chabot, who had not forgotten the abuse showered upon him by Henry and Cromwell early in the spring, and who had been further angered by the execution of the Carthusian priors just before the conference at Calais began. The conference having been broken up, Chabot left Calais in a very bad temper on 14 June.

The failure of Norfolk and his colleagues had an unhappy effect on the fate of the prisoners in the Tower. After the victory of Anne in February, they had been kept in somewhat closer confinement, but at first they had not been otherwise molested. When Cromwell recovered from his illness, and active measures were taken against the adherents of the pope, they suffered from the change. On 30 April, the day after the Charterhouse monks were condemned to die, More was called before some of the royal councillors and warned that if he did not give way he might incur the same penalties as the Carthusians. But his fortitude was not to be shaken; he refused to yield. On 4 May he was again examined, and admonished not to expose himself to the fate of those who had just been led to execution. Subsequently, More, Bishop Fisher, Dr Abel, the former chaplain of Catherine, and Featherstone, Mary's former schoolmaster, were formally called upon to submit within six weeks; otherwise, they would be put upon their trial.

They might still have escaped had not the suspicions of the king been aroused by the resolute tone of the French and by the rashness of the pope. The French admiral at Calais had persisted in speaking of Princess Mary; Morette assiduously cultivated the good will of Chapuis; and Morette's servants talked very freely about the marriage of Mary and the dauphin. Henry began to fear that the proposals made by Count Henry of Nassau, of which Chabot had given him warning, had been secretly accepted by France, and that Francis would try to get possession of Mary in order to make her the dauphin's wife.

The news from Rome was still more disquieting. The papal court had, of course, been informed of the disfavour into which Anne had fallen at the end of 1534, and of the extreme insecurity of her position during the first two months of 1535. Paul III then hoped that Henry, cured of his passion for Anne, would retrace his steps; and the Cardinal of Lorraine, the most influential of all the cardinals of the French faction, promised, as we have seen, to go to England to bring about a reconciliation. There seemed to be little doubt that if the cardinal fulfilled his promise, Henry would submit, as it was inconceivable that he would insult Francis by refusing the mediation of so great a man. The cardinal, however, did not go; his place was taken by Chabot; and when the pope complained, it was replied that equally good results might be obtained at the meeting at Calais. Paul III greatly doubted this, but he did not doubt that the French and Gregorio da Casale were right in the accounts they gave him of a change in Henry's temper and convictions. The pope was not aware that there had been a reaction, that Anne was once more triumphant, and that the favourable opportunity had been lost. Believing that Fisher, who had been so leniently treated at the beginning of the year, continued to enjoy the favour of the king, he allowed himself to be persuaded to make the good bishop a cardinal. This was done on 21 May; and Jean du Bellay, Henry's stout friend and advocate, and Girolamo Ghinucci, his former ambassador, were also – at the same consistory – promoted to the dignity of the purple.

As soon as Gregorio da Casale heard of the creation, he strongly protested against it. The pope began to think that he had made a mistake, but as it was now past remedy, he tried to excuse what he had done, saying he had hoped to please rather than to offend the King of England. Casale, fearing that Henry would suspect him of having advised the nomination of Fisher, and that he might lose his pension, asked that at least the red hat should not be sent to Fisher; but this request seems to have been disregarded. Shortly afterwards the French ambassador, Charles de Denonville, Bishop of Mâcon, received letters about the execution of the Carthusian monks; and when they were read in consistory, they dispelled any illusion which the pope or the cardinals may still have retained as to Henry's intentions.

Paul III, now seriously alarmed, sent for Denonville, and asked him to beg Francis to intercede for the new cardinal. The ambassador, while promising to write to the king, gave little hope. The imperialists, he said, in order to make Henry suspicious of the good faith of Francis, were pretending that the honour had been granted on the recommendation of the French. If Francis pleaded for Fisher, Henry would probably believe what the imperial agents asserted, and resent his intervention. Paul III was greatly distressed, and once more protested that he had not intended to displease King Henry. He was ready, he declared, to give a written attestation that he had never been asked by any prince to confer the cardinal's hat on the Bishop of Rochester.

The Bishop of Mâcon wrote to his master and to Cardinal du Bellay; and Nicolas Raince, the French permanent secretary, also wrote at the urgent request of the pope. Moreover, in two letters addressed to du Bellay, Gregorio da Casale proposed that Fisher should promise, if his life were spared, to swear to the statutes in order to be allowed to go to Rome to receive the red hat. This would be very advantageous to Henry, who would be glad to get rid of his opponent. Casale did not say that the scheme had been approved of by the pope, but he had no doubt that Paul III would absolve Fisher from any sin he might commit in taking the oath.

It is most unlikely that Fisher would ever have condescended to save his life by a subterfuge such as Casale suggested; he was not the man to forswear himself, even if he had the secret permission of the pope to do so. But he does not appear to have been put to the test. On receiving the letters of Denonville, Francis asked Henry to spare Fisher's life, and, if Cardinal du Bellay is to be trusted, Henry answered that the request should be granted; but, whatever promise the king may have made, he had no mind to fulfil it. He was in an angry and suspicious mood. Not only had the pope dared to confer a high dignity on a rebellious subject of his, but Jean du Bellay, who had seemed to be almost a Protestant, and whom he had always expected to help him in inciting Francis to open rebellion against the papacy, had accepted the red hat. Henry regarded such conduct as little short of treason.

Besides, Gregorio da Casale had written to Cromwell that it was the French who, after the execution of the Carthusians, had spoken most passionately of Henry's cruelty. This confirmed Henry in his belief that he was betrayed by Francis, and that a great league had been formed against him. He felt like an animal at bay, and as he could not touch the pope, or the King of France, or the Bishop of Paris, he resolved to wreak his vengeance on the prisoners in the Tower.

Henry felt convinced that Fisher had corresponded with the pope, and that his promotion was a part of some vast scheme of the opposition. He considered the bishop his greatest enemy, and believed him to be far more dangerous than in any circumstances he could have been. When the news of Fisher's elevation had arrived, Henry had broken out into violent threats, and had immediately sent a commission to the Tower to find whether the honour had been asked for. The cardinal asserted that the pope had acted of his own free will, but this did not satisfy the king. Several of the jailers and some friends and kinsmen of Fisher were arrested on a charge of having served as his messengers, and were closely examined. Of course, nothing to their disadvantage was proved, but still the king was not mollified.

On the 14th a royal commission again examined Fisher and More, and demanded that they should accept the Acts of Succession and of Supremacy.Both refused to make any statement. Thereupon an indictment was prepared against the cardinal, and on 17 June he was brought to trial at Westminster. His rights as a peer were disregarded, the government holding that by the Act of Attainder passed in the autumn of 1534, he had been deprived of his see and of the honour attached to it. A common jury it was easy to pack and easy to frighten, so a sentence for the crown was obtained, and five days later Fisher was led to execution on Tower Hill. The extreme penalty of treason had been commuted into simple decapitation, and even on the scaffold a pardon was offered to him if he would submit. He remained firm, spoke a few words to the assembled crowd, laid his head on the block, and received the stroke of the axe. The king had ordered one of the preachers of the modern school to be his confessor, and even this man, prejudiced as he must have been against Fisher, was loud in praise of his goodness and sanctity.

Meanwhile, Anne did her best to divert Henry's attention from his embarrassments. She organised splendid balls and mummeries, and by cleverly playing, now on his obstinacy, now on his vanity and love of show, she established her old empire over his vacillating mind. It was not, therefore, difficult for the Boleyn party to persuade him that Sir Thomas More should also be brought to trial. On 26 June a true bill was found against Sir Thomas by the grand jury for Middlesex, and on 1 July he was led to Westminster Hall to be tried before a special commission. He offered an eloquent defence, but it could not have any influence on the jury; he was found guilty, and sentenced to receive the punishment of a traitor. A few days later he was executed, maintaining to the last the quaint humour, the delicate tenderness, the stainless honour, which, with his fine intellectual genius, make him one of the noblest and most attractive figures in English history.

With this last and most illustrious victim Henry's cruelties, for the moment, came to an end. It soon became apparent that the executions would not have the effect which he had desired and expected. More and Fisher enjoyed so high a fame for piety, virtue and learning that their death roused a storm of indignation. In England, indeed, most people were afraid to say what they thought, but abroad Henry was loudly and universally condemned. Francis I spoke very strongly to Sir John Wallop, the English ambassador, and he might have spoken more strongly still had he not known that Wallop was at heart deeply displeased. The French ministers expressed themselves with even greater freedom than their master.

At Rome the French cardinals no longer opposed the publication of the sentence against Henry. Even Cardinal du Bellay ceased to defend him, and sought only to exonerate Francis from blame for the relations that had hitherto been maintained between France and England. Consistories and congregations met, therefore, to prepare a bull of deprivation and excommunication; and decisive measures would have been taken had not the imperial agents at the papal court suddenly realised that there were formidable obstacles in the way. They sent a long memoir to the emperor setting forth their difficulties, and asking what they were to do.

The pope and the cardinals, they said, shocked by the execution of the Cardinal of Rochester, wished to deprive Henry of his throne for the crimes of heresy and *lesæ majestatis*, England being still reputed at Rome to be held in fief of the Holy See. But if this were done, the kingdom would revert to the pope as feudal overlord, and Princess Mary would lose her rights. The deprivation might, indeed, be made in favour of Mary, but such an arrangement could not be kept secret; the new cardinals would divulge it; and Henry might treat the princess as he had treated Cardinal Fisher. Upon the whole, it seemed best that the pope should deprive Henry without saying in whose favour he acted; and then the imperial agents might appear for

Catherine and Mary, and claim the vacant throne for the latter. But as every conceivable plan would be attended with danger, they did not dare to come to a final resolution without further instructions.

The result of all this was that the bull of deprivation was not issued. But the indignation against the King of England remained as strong as ever, and the only question now was whether the pope was likely to find a secular prince able and willing to carry out his sentence.

Henry was regarded with hardly less hostility by the majority of foreign Protestants than by Roman Catholics. There had always been a radical distinction between the English and the Continental reformation. The German theologians who broke away from Rome, admitting no authority but that of the Scripture, could not favour a theory of royal supremacy, which if generally acknowledged would have set up, instead of one pope, hundreds of popes. They disliked Henry's proceedings, and feared that he would permanently discredit their cause. For political reasons he had favoured Wullenwever, who was strongly suspected of Protestant heterodoxy; and there is reason to think that he was at least very near entering into negotiations with the Anabaptists at Muenster, who pleased him by giving constant trouble to Mary of Hungary, the regent of the Low Countries. Henry knew how much he was distrusted by moderate Protestants; and, to vindicate his character, he had caused a number of Anabaptists, who had fled from Holland to England, to be arrested in May, and to be brought before a commission. Fourteen of them had refused to retract, and had been burned as heretics. This did not conciliate the German reformers, who continued to suspect Henry of being friendly to John of Leyden.

The execution of Fisher and More widened the breach between Henry and the Lutherans. Both men had been firm opponents of English Protestantism, but they had also been personal friends of the foremost Humanists; and they themselves had been among the principal representatives in England of the new learning, on which the German reformation was chiefly based. Like Luther, Fisher maintained the validity of Catherine's marriage, not because he believed in the power of the pope to dispense from a prescription in the Bible, but because he held that there was no prescription of the kind to be found in the Bible;and in matters about which public opinion was divided this was by no means the only important point on which they agreed. Fisher, therefore, was respected by Luther's followers, while for Sir Thomas More they had the strongest admiration; and the tidings that two such men had been beheaded filled them with astonishment and horror.

Seeing how violent a commotion he had produced, Henry became anxious to justify himself for what he had done. Several memorials were drawn up in defence of his conduct, and in one of them, which was evidently intended for the Roman Catholics, especially for the French, the following passage occurs:

First, to assaye the mind of the most Christian majesty (oh, subtle craft!) concerning the deliverance of the late bishop of Rochester being in the ende for his unfeigned deserving condemned of treason, whom they after his death (and God's will), to excite the hatred of all cardinals, name a cardinal, he [the pope] does say that the labour of the most Christian majesty interposed with his brother the most noble king of England, was contemned, set at nought, and mocked; where indeed no such labour was made. And yet that holy see not content with that lie makes another open lie and most falsely brings in that the intercession of the most Christian majesty has caused the said Rochester to die the rather. In this matter I call to record the conscience of the most Christian majesty, which, forsomuch as he never inter… with his friend in this cause (of whom he knows he may obtain anything that he desires) not only does see most manifestly now their lies, but also (such is his prudence) he has plainly declared that he hates all treason and inobedience, in so much that he thought that there should be given no place to … neither prayer in such case for the maintenance of the commonwealth in his estate.

Especial credit is taken for the manner in which Fisher was put to death:

He was not killed with poison, which thing some men do use, he was not sodden in lead as the solemn use is in certain places, he was not hanged in a halter, what best agrees for a traitor, he was not burnt, he was not put to death with lingering torments, but lost his life with a sudden stroke of a sworde the which sort of death in such bitterness is most easy.

This memorial was conceived with much skill, for Francis could not afford to say that he had in vain interfered for Fisher. That would detract from his reputation by showing that he had little influence in England. On the other hand, by remaining silent, he would seem to admit that he had approved of Fisher's execution, since it would be said that if he had not approved of it, he – Henry's greatest friend – would surely have tried to prevent it. The dilemma was a most unpleasant one, and Francis was indignant with Henry for forcing it upon him.

Another memorial, which seems to have been drawn up somewhat later, was intended to allay the indignation of the German Protestants; and in this production, which is in Latin, a virulent attack is made on the character of the dead men. 'As you write', the paper begins:

> that everywhere in Germany the king is believed to have punished More and Rochester for no other cause than that they sincerely adhered to evangelical doctrine and persistently opposed the king's marriage, we wonder who can be the author of this idle tale.

The king's beneficence, equity, piety and mildness were so well known to the world that his reputation for these qualities could not be easily undermined by calumny. With what exquisite kindness he had treated King James of Scotland, not holding him responsible for the atrocious misdeeds of his father! What generosity he had shown to Francis I, to whom, out of pure goodness, he had lent 800,000 crowns towards his ransom! The king never prevented the gospel from being preached if it were preached truly and honestly. Why, then, this impudent calumny that More and Rochester were punished because they sincerely adhered to evangelical doctrine and opposed the king's marriage? No one had been more willing than they to swear to the Acts by which the crown was settled on the offspring of Henry and Anne; and More, in his dialogues against Luther, had contended that marriages prohibited in Leviticus are not permitted to Christians. As for what was said about their defence of the gospel, the writer wondered whether any German believed that the gospel had ever had enemies more mischievous than these two. Rochester and More had both written books in which they had bitterly assailed the best leaders of the sect; and in a letter to

Erasmus, More had openly stated that he would be a constant enemy of heretics, for so he called those who wanted a purer doctrine. And so he had shown himself. 'It makes one ashamed,' says this virtuous scribe, 'to recall what tortures he invented and inflicted upon those whom he perceived to be inclined to evangelical truth.' He caused search to be made in all quarters for heretics, offering great rewards for evidence against them; and when they were brought before him, he never committed them to prison 'until he had seen them tortured in a pitiable manner before his eyes'. That More was 'of a cruel and fierce temper' might be judged from this fact, that those whom he caught 'he was in the habit of torturing by a new method invented by himself'. He immediately caused new shoes to be put upon persons brought before him; then the victims were tied to stakes, and the soles of their feet were brought close to a blazing fire, that, to those who would not confess, the pain – . Here, unhappily, a sheet of the manuscript has been lost. The document closes with a prayer that all princes may be able to imitate Henry's immense goodness of heart. These accusations against More have been repeated by some later writers; but there is not a tittle of evidence that he was guilty of the cruelties imputed to him. Such charges conflict with all that we know of his character and his modes of thought; and to his contemporaries they were absolutely incredible. Henry gained nothing by the attempt to tarnish the fame of one whose virtues were so widely known and so cordially appreciated.

4

The Ambassadors & International Affairs

The extreme unpopularity of Anne and of her kinsfolk and friends did not escape the notice of the ambassadors. The common people, they reported, were extremely angry against Anne, abusing her in no measured terms for the danger and distress into which she had brought the country. The upper classes were nearly all equally bitter, some on account of the changes in religion, others for fear of war and of ruin to trade, others, and by far the greater number, from loyalty to Catherine and Mary. Englishmen had no wish to see Elizabeth on the throne, with Anne Boleyn and Lord Rochford as her guardians and as regents during a long minority.

Anne herself was fully conscious of the difficulties of her position. To one of the gentlemen who accompanied Dinteville, the French ambassador, she granted a private audience, and he reported to Marguerite of Navarre the substance of their conversation. Anne said that the two things she most desired on earth were to have a son and to meet Queen Marguerite once more. She seemed ill at ease and harassed, and the eagerness with which she wished to be recommended to Marguerite showed how much she wanted sympathy and help.

In proof of the great popularity of Mary the ambassador mentioned the following curious fact. When Mary had left Greenwich to go to Eltham, a great many women, in spite of their husbands, had flocked to see her pass, and had cheered her, calling out that, notwithstanding all laws to the contrary, she was still their princess. Several of them, being of higher rank than the rest, had been arrested, and, as they had proved obstinate, had been sent to the Tower. On the margin of that part of the report in which this circumstance is recorded we find the words, written by Dinteville himself: 'Note, my Lord Rochford and my Lord William.' The ambassador clearly meant that Lady Rochford, Anne's sister-in-law, and Lady William Howard were among those who had cheered Mary. We know from Chapuis that Lady Rochford had in the preceding autumn been sent from court, but the imperial ambassador ascribed her disgrace to intrigues on behalf of, not in opposition to, Anne. Had Lady Rochford's absence from court produced a change? That may have been so, for it is said that towards the end of the year she was on bad terms with her husband. Lady William Howard was certainly hostile to Anne, and she and Lady Rochford were great friends. Dinteville may therefore have been right.

Considering the difficulties of the government, the temper of the nation, and the supposed inclination of Mary, the French ambassadors came to the conclusion that a marriage between the dauphin and the princess might be brought about more easily than had been expected. They proposed that Paul III should be told of the offers which had been made to Francis by Henry on condition that Francis would throw off his allegiance to the Holy See, and make war on the emperor. The pope should be warned, they suggested, that if war broke out it might be necessary to accept these offers, and that then he would lose his revenues from France as he had lost his revenues from England. The ambassadors believed that to prevent so unholy an alliance Paul III would ask the emperor himself to propose the marriage, and that Charles, for the sake of his aunt and his cousin, might be persuaded to do so. If he consented, Henry would of course be immediately informed of the fact, and the French king might tell Henry that war would be unavoidable unless the proposal were accepted. Anne would oppose the marriage, but Henry would be afraid to offend both the king and the emperor. Besides, Anne's influence was on the wane; the king had again changed his mistress.

Feeling sure that Henry would have to give way, the French ambassadors were not at all careful to hide their opinions and their wishes. They permitted their servants to talk openly of the advantages which would arise from the marriage of the dauphin and the princess, and some indignation was caused by this freedom of discourse, for Henry was certain that if he consented to the marriage he would soon have a very precarious hold on the loyalty of his subjects. Perceiving the danger, he was angry with his former friends for trying to increase it and to profit by his difficulties.

Cromwell also was extremely angry with the French. At heart he was rather favourable to Mary, and of late his relations with Anne had not always been very good; but as he had no wish to see England become a dependency of France, he resisted the proposed match and stood loyally by Henry and Anne against the peril which was threatening them. With the French ambassadors he had been for some time on bad terms. On 29 June the Bishop of Tarbes and Morette had invited him to dinner, but he had rudely refused, saying that he knew what they wanted to tell him, and that he did not wish to hear it. Shortly afterwards he had an angry discussion with the ambassadors, whom he treated with considerable insolence; and when they resented his arrogance, he used his influence to prevent the bishop from being lodged, as most of his predecessors had been, at the king's cost at Bridewell.

The English ministers, being in ill humour with the French, tried to convey the impression that their relations with the emperor were improving. A new ambassador, Richard Pate, had been appointed to reside with Charles V; and Cromwell and his colleagues went about talking of the honour with which he had been received at the imperial court. Henry himself considerably altered his tone, no longer speaking of the ingratitude of Charles, but, on the contrary, praising him. Towards Chapuis the English ministers made a great show of cordiality. They offered him all kinds of little favours, and frequently sent for him to discuss the most unimportant matters, hoping to make the English public and the French ambassadors believe that important negotiations were going on.

The proposals made by the English ministers for the purpose of regaining the friendship of the emperor were considered by Chapuis quite unacceptable. The negotiation which Sir John Wallop had begun with Viscount Hanart in Paris had led to no result, for Henry would not consent to treat Catherine and Mary with royal honours, as the emperor desired; and by the execution of the Carthusians, of Fisher, and of More, he had shown how he intended to behave towards the friends of the queen and the princess. Cromwell had suggested that a marriage might be concluded between Philip, the son of the emperor, and the little Lady Elizabeth; but, brazen-faced as he was, even Cromwell dared not press this scheme, and Chapuis contemptuously ignored all references to it. He remained coldly distant, waiting for an occasion when he might advise his master to act for Catherine and Mary with vigour.

The French party at the English court was so discredited that Anne had bitter quarrels with her uncle, the Duke of Norfolk, and, about Christmas 1534, abused him in unmeasured terms. The Duke left her presence in anger, and in the hall spoke against her with indecent violence. Shortly afterwards he retired from the court, thus relieving Cromwell of all fear of serious opposition in the royal council. But Anne was not yet satisfied, and seized every opportunity to bring her uncle into disgrace.

International relations being so unsatisfactory, the country became more and more discontented, and Cromwell could not venture to act with his wonted energy and fearlessness. The taxes which had been granted by parliament he was unable to levy, for fear of exasperating the people; yet the royal coffers were empty, not only because the French pensions were withheld, but because, owing to the bad harvest, the farmers on the royal domains could not pay their rents. The result was that the salaries of officials were not paid, and that the whole machinery of administration began to go out of gear. The government was already despoiling small convents, the heads of houses being brought by bribes, threats, and insults to acquiesce in the dissolution of their communities. But the lands and other possessions obtained in this way brought in only a small immediate return in ready money or in things that could be at once exchanged for ready money; and the advantages of confiscation, such as they were, were dearly purchased at the cost of much popular irritation.

Altogether, Henry's position was not at this time an enviable one. When he looked around him, he saw his people thoroughly disaffected, the pope exasperated and striving to raise against him as many enemies as possible, the King of France negotiating with the emperor for the purpose of dethroning him, the Protestant princes of Germany offended and deeply suspicious, and the fleets of Sweden, Denmark, and Prussia capturing and pillaging his ships.

Henry did not underrate his difficulties, nor did he hide from himself that most of them had sprung from the policy necessitated by his union with Anne. He fondly believed that the hatred of his subjects was mainly directed against her, and that if she were not in his way he might still triumph over his enemies. As he thought of this, the idea of discarding Anne rose before his mind even more vividly than it had done at the beginning of the year; and the idea was certainly not rendered less attractive by the fact that Anne, worn out by constant exertion and anxiety, had lost her good looks. Even to Margaret Shelton, who had so recently touched his fancy, he was already becoming indifferent. During the summer he had gone on progress through the south-western counties; and on 10 September the court had been at Wolfhall, in Wiltshire, the seat of Sir John Seamer or Seymour, father of Mistress Jane Seymour, a former attendant of Queen Catherine. Whether it was on this occasion that Henry began to pay attention to his future queen is not certain, but a few weeks later the French ambassadors reported that the king had a new love.

Although Henry might be heartily tired of Anne, he remembered the advice given him in February when he had first spoken of discarding her. He must either keep her or take Catherine back. Was this the only conceivable alternative? No; Catherine might die; and if she were dead, Henry would not only be rid of his most energetic opponent, the woman to whose influence the resistance of Mary seemed chiefly due, he would be free to separate his fortunes from those of Anne.

For the last two years Henry and his ministers had spoken of the death of Catherine as an event that would soon happen. One day Gregorio da Casale told Chapuis that Henry had said she had the dropsy and in a short time would die of it. Chapuis remarked that the queen had never suffered from anything like dropsy; and he vehemently suspected that the prediction of her approaching death meant that she was to be poisoned. The friends of Catherine and Mary had been warned that Anne wished to poison her rivals. Dr Ortiz had been told in Rome by the auditor Simonetta that this was her purpose. The Earl of Northumberland, who at the time was still on friendly terms with Anne, made a similar communication to a gentleman at court, who reported it to Chapuis. Pope Clement VII, after he had delivered sentence in March 1534, had expressed a fear that the result might be the death of the queen. Anne herself spoke in a violent strain. In the summer of 1534 she plainly said that she intended to kill Mary during Henry's absence from England; and in March 1535, when she regained her ascendancy, she was reported to have suborned a man to pretend that God had revealed to him that while the princess dowager and the Lady Mary lived Queen Anne would bear no children to the king. About the same time she denounced the two ladies as rebels and traitors who merited death; and after the execution of Fisher and More she directly urged Henry to inflict the same penalty on Catherine and Mary, saying that they deserved death even more than those who had just been beheaded. The hatred she had conceived for them blinded her to her own real interests.

Cromwell did not hate the queen and the princess; but he thought that if they were out of the way he would be able to compose the differences between Henry and Charles, and to avert the danger of a foreign invasion. And he made no secret of his feelings. In August 1534, he said to one of the lords that the Low Countries were too much afraid of losing their commerce to allow the emperor to make war upon England. 'But even if this were not the case,' he added, 'the death of Catherine and Mary would prevent any rupture, for then there would be no occasion for a quarrel.' In March 1535, he asked Chapuis what evil or danger would arise from the death of the princess, even if it excited the indignation of the people, and what cause the emperor would have to be offended by it. The ambassador gave an angry reply, having no wish to hear dark speeches which might lead to even darker deeds. But a few weeks afterwards Cromwell spoke again in the same sense, declaring that Mary was at the root of all the king's perplexities. 'And,' he added, 'I pray God... ' Here he stopped, but, as Chapuis remarked, it was not necessary to finish the sentence; his meaning was clear enough.

Henry had also begun to talk in a rather ominous way. Mary having fallen ill, he went to Greenwich, where she was then staying; and in the presence of all the servants he loudly ordered Lady Shelton to tell her ward that she was his worst enemy, and that on her account he was on bad terms with most of the princes of Christendom. Chapuis interpreted this message as an encouragement to those who might feel inclined to poison the princess.

During the latter half of 1533 and during the whole of 1534, Chapuis credited Anne and her friends with the most infamous designs. For the protection of Mary against certain dangers at which he occasionally hinted in his letters to the emperor, and to Granvelle and his son, he could trust only to the virtue and firmness of Mary herself. But for her protection against attempts to poison her he took active measures. For some time he wished that she should reside with her mother, but this was refused, and in the end it seemed to him best that they should not live together; for if Mary stayed with her mother her enemies might poison her without exciting suspicion, whereas if she was with Lady Shelton they could not harm her without immediately causing a popular outcry. Having arrived at this conviction, Chapuis tried to help the princess by influencing her guardian. He sent Lady Shelton little presents with complimentary messages, but at the same time gave her to understand that she herself would be in the greatest danger if the princess died while entrusted to her charge. In the spring of 1535 Doctor William Butt, the royal physician, was ordered to attend the princess; and he assisted the ambassador by telling Lady Shelton that it was commonly reported in London that she had poisoned Mary. The poor lady was not a little frightened, and whenever Mary was ill cried bitterly and was in the utmost anxiety.

Catherine did not seem to be in the same imminent danger as her daughter. With a few of her own servants and a large staff of royal officials, she had remained at Bugden until the spring of 1534, when she had been conveyed to Kimbolton, near Huntingdon. She had been several times annoyed by commissioners calling upon her to swear to the new Acts and threatening her with the penalties for high treason; but in the autumn of 1534 she had enjoyed a short time of quiet. When, however, the young lady who had worked in her favour lost the good graces of the king, she was again treated as harshly as before, and in the summer and the autumn of 1535 she bitterly complained of the cruelty of her oppressors.

The only servants of Catherine at Kimbolton, besides her female attendants, were George de Atequa, Bishop of Llandaff, her confessor; Miguel de Lasco, her physician; Juan de Soto, her apothecary; Philip Grenacre, de Soto's assistant; and Francisco Phelipe, her groom of the chamber. The royal servants, under the command of Sir Edward Chamberlain and Sir Edmund Bedingfield were far more numerous.

They acted as the garrison of the castle, as the queen's gaolers, and as spies upon her conduct and upon that of her attendants. She could not leave the house without permission; and when permission was granted, she had to accept the company of royal officers, who prevented her from communicating with the people. Visitors were not admitted except by special order from the king or from Cromwell, and her letters had to be smuggled in and out by her Spanish servants.

In the summer of 1534 Chapuis had asked Cromwell for a warrant to see the queen; and having waited for some time without obtaining a reply, he had set out with a large train for Kimbolton. While he was on the road, a royal messenger passed him, riding post-haste; and shortly afterwards he received a message from Chamberlain and Bedingfield that by the king's orders he would neither be admitted to the castle nor allowed to speak with the queen. After some discussion the ambassador returned to London, but not before a part of his retinue had gone close to Kimbolton, where they spoke with Catherine's attendants, some of whom were standing on the battlements, while others looked out of the windows.

By such protests and demonstrations Chapuis hoped to counteract the sinister advice given to the king, and as time went on and the two ladies were neither poisoned nor brought to trial, he became less anxious. He was told that the king had no wish to hurt either of them, but intended to keep them as hostages for his own safety; and Chapuis believed what he was told, and ceased to pay much attention to floating rumours on the subject. Early in November 1535, his confidence was rudely disturbed.

5

Catherine's Death & Jane Seymour

On the second of May following Catherine's death, Anne Boleyn was arrested. That same evening, when the Duke of Richmond, Henry's bastard son, was saying good night to his father, the king burst into tears. 'The duke and his sister, the Lady Mary,' exclaimed Henry, 'might thank God for having escaped the hands of that damned poisonous wretch who had conspired their death.' And shortly afterwards, at the trial of Anne, the royal officers laid it to the charge of the prisoner that she was strongly suspected of having caused the late princess dowager to be poisoned, and of having intended to do the same by the Lady Mary. A scapegoat having been found, Henry's ministers did not deny that Catherine had been murdered.

With so formidable a mass of evidence it cannot but seem likely that Catherine met with foul play. If such was the case, the poison was probably administered twice in small doses, at the end of November and shortly after Christmas. Poisoning by repeated low doses was thought by the great toxicologists of the sixteenth century to be preferable to every other method. Usually the victim did not die of the direct effect of the poison, but of exhaustion caused by frequent illnesses; so that, as a rule, no traces of the drug were found in the body, and the course of the disorder did not present those strong and characteristic symptoms which might otherwise have appeared. Thus poisoners were able to baffle the efforts of the most skilful physicians, and in most cases to prevent the detection of their crime.

If a murder was committed, it is for the present impossible to say who was the actual murderer, or whose immediate orders he obeyed.

The accusation brought by the royal officers in May against Anne Boleyn may have been well founded. Chapuis thought her guilty, and so did others; but Chapuis equally accused the king, and from what we know he had good reason to do so. The behaviour of Henry II towards Thomas a Becket was not worse than that of Henry VIII towards Catherine, and historians are generally agreed in saying that Henry II prompted a murder.

On the king, who made the death of Catherine a political necessity, rests the responsibility for what may have been done, not on those who in their own way fulfilled his command. Anne Boleyn may have contributed to the result, her advice may have strengthened the king in his opinion, and may have encouraged those by whom the crime was directly ordered. But the attempt to throw the whole blame on her shoulders was an attempt to exonerate the principal culprit. Her guilt, whatever it may have been, was less than that of Henry, for she was bound by no tie to the queen, and she did to Catherine what would have been done to her had Catherine possessed the power.

On receiving the letter of Chamberlain and Bedingfield which announced Catherine's death, Cromwell immediately wrote to the Bishop of Winchester and Sir John Wallop, the English ambassadors at the French court. He instructed them to communicate the good news to Francis, and in their negotiations to modify their action in accordance with the new order of things. But before he had time to send off the letter, he received a message from Henry directing him to point out to the ambassadors that, Catherine being dead, there was no longer any reason to apprehend the hostility of the emperor. This they were to explain to the French, and Francis was to be warned that he might be forestalled by Charles V if he did not at once accept Henry's proposals. If, notwithstanding this warning, Francis still required the ambassadors to abate their claims, they were to show themselves unwilling to do so. It is quite clear that Henry fully understood how much his position had been bettered by the death of his wife, and how much less he depended on the goodwill of France.

A few days after Dinteville had left England the Bishop of Winchester had been sent to assist and perhaps to watch Sir John Wallop at the French court. The choice was not a happy one, for Gardiner had made himself unpopular with the French by his overbearing temper, and by the part he had taken in the intrigues at Marseilles. Probably he was chosen as much because at home they wished to be rid of him as because he was considered a very fit instrument. At the French court he met with little success. The demands of France were as exorbitant as ever, and Gardiner quickly perceived that there was scarcely any chance of an agreement. But a few days after his arrival news came from Italy which raised a hope that the French would attribute more importance to the friendship of Henry, and that they might be brought to make considerable concessions.

Maximilian Sforza, the Duke of Milan, had died without issue; and Francis, who had always pretended a title to the duchy, now claimed the succession. He at once asked the emperor to give investiture of the duchy to Henry, Duke of Orleans, his second son. To this Charles demurred, for Henry of Orleans, next to the dauphin, who was of feeble health and unmarried, was at this time heir to the French crown; and if he were made Duke of Milan, and if his elder brother died childless, the duchy would belong to the King of France, who would thus obtain a strong hold over upper and central Italy. Moreover, Henry of Orleans, in virtue of his wife, Catherine dei Medici, thought he had some claim to the Duchy of Urbino, Camerino, and other places in the Romagna. If he obtained possession of Milan, he would try to enforce his pretensions; so that the emperor, instead of securing peace by the concession demanded of him by Francis, would be involved in new quarrels and new wars.

But while Charles would not grant Milan to Henry of Orleans, he was ready to make sacrifices in order to avoid a war with France. The Tunisian expedition had been rather expensive; and Khairredin, although beaten and driven from one of his strongholds, had been able to retain Algiers, and had reconstituted a fleet with which he was once more threatening the shores and islands of Spain and Italy. The emperor was, therefore, really anxious to maintain peace with France, and in the hope that a compromise might be accepted he offered to give the investiture of Milan to the third son of Francis, the Duke of Angoulême. Negotiations were begun for the fulfilment of this plan, the pope did his best to mediate, and the moderate party in France were favourable to an understanding.

The English ambassadors watched these negotiations with keen interest, and strove to counteract them, making common cause with the admiral of France, who was at the head of the war party, and with the Italian refugees, who wished to return to their country and estates by the force of French arms. Gardiner and Wallop promised Francis some subsidies if he would invade Italy, and with the help of Chabot they prevailed over the moderate party. As a preliminary for further operations, Francis sent the Count de Saint Pol with a strong force to invade Bresse and Savoy up to the Alps. He assisted the malcontents at Geneva, who had driven out their bishop and the officials of the duke, and he urged the Swiss to overrun the Pays de Vaud. Thus, before the new year, Charles of Savoy was deprived of nearly all his lands on the western side of the Alps.

The emperor, who fully understood that this was but the beginning of a far more serious war, set himself to prepare for the worst. He tried to gain the pope over by making great offers to his son, Pier Luigi Farnese, and endeavoured to unite the smaller Italian states in a general confederacy for the protection of the Duke of Savoy and the defence of Italy. Best of all, new troops were raised in Germany and Italy to reinforce the army the emperor had brought back from Tunis. In Spain, the Low Countries, and Italy, everything was made ready to repel an attack by the French in the coming spring.

These signs of an approaching storm were observed by Henry with unfeigned delight. He thought that if war broke out Francis would be less overbearing, and thankful for any assistance England might give him, while the emperor would no longer dare to favour the English malcontents. Even if the latter anticipation proved to be mistaken, Henry was persuaded that Charles would be unable to do him any harm. He was confident that the struggle between his lukewarm friend and his staunch opponent would be an excellent safeguard for his own tranquillity.

Henry altogether misapprehended the influences which were likely to determine Charles's course. Hitherto the emperor had been held back from active interference in favour of Catherine and Mary chiefly by the fear that any attempt of the kind would occasion a rupture with France. If for other reasons he were compelled once more to fight Francis, the principal cause of his hesitation would be removed. No sooner, therefore, did war seem to be unavoidable than he began to think rather seriously about giving the English malcontents the aid they asked for. In December, after the invasion of the territory of the

Duke of Savoy by St Pol, he all but decided to assist the English lords; and an important preliminary step was taken.

Charles did not rely on the assurances of the malcontents that in case of insurrection Mary would be in no danger. He could not feel quite sure as to Kingston's loyalty to her and to the queen; and he feared a sudden outbreak of rage on the part of the king. Besides, he wished to be able to set up Mary as a pretender against Henry; and it appeared to him necessary that she should be in some place where he could constantly communicate with her. After the death of Fisher and More, Mary had repeatedly urged Chapuis to procure for her the means of flight, but the ambassador, bound by his instructions, did not dare to proceed any further in the matter. Now Charles V himself took the initiative. The Count de Roeulx, his captain-general in the Low Countries, was commissioned to send a special agent to England to prepare for Mary's flight. If all went well, the princess was to be carried off in February, and in March or April the insurrection was to follow. Shortly after the new year, Roeulx's agent arrived in England, and he and Chapuis carefully considered how Mary could be safely carried away.

This was only one of many difficulties in which Henry was now entangled. In November Sir Francis Bryan had been sent to help Gardiner and Wallop in their negotiations with the French; and in the beginning of December he had met the court near Pargaix, the country seat of Chabot de Brion. Here, immediately after Bryan's arrival, the three ambassadors were told by the ministers of Francis of some despatches which had just been received from Rome. They contained a copy of the sentence of excommunication and deprivation against Henry VIII which had been drawn up by order of the pope. It had been read in the middle of November in consistory, and Cardinal du Bellay, who was at Rome, had forwarded a copy of it to Francis I. The cardinal expressed his belief that there would never be another sentence like it. 'We are well aware', he continued:

that it is necessary for you that the sentence should be in any case a very severe one, but there are some articles so expressly designed for you that a blind man would see that they have been inserted for no other purpose than to compel you to lose either the pope or the King of England.

Du Bellay added that he and the Bishop of Mâcon would do their best to gain time until they should hear from Francis, but that they had little hope of succeeding.

Francis now found himself in a very perplexing position. If he chose to stand by Henry, he would drive the pope into the arms of Charles; and he knew, of course, that nothing could be more detrimental to his interests in Italy, which were at this moment engrossing his attention. On the other hand, if Francis wished to obtain the goodwill of the pope, he would have to give up his alliance with Henry. The difficulty was in part explained to the English ambassadors, who knew not what to do. Bryan decided that he would not declare his charge to Francis until he and Gardiner received fresh instructions.

Henry received the news with astonishment and anger. He had never doubted that the death of Sforza would make the French more desirous of securing his friendship, and to his dismay he found that this was not the case. Some contemptuous expressions used by the admiral of France about his power greatly enraged him, and he instructed Gardiner and Wallop strongly to protest against them. He appears to have been really convinced that he possessed formidable power, and that he ought to have been taken more seriously into account.

According to his wont, Henry exaggerated his own importance. He was held in very small esteem, and every prince who had anything to lose shrank from an alliance with a king who might be deposed the day after the treaty was signed. His duplicity had been so great that nobody would rely on his assurances or accept his offers without good guarantees.

Even now he was doing what he could to destroy the last remnant of good-will which the members of the Schmalkaldic League might feel for him. In the beginning of November, after having been arrested, Juergen Wullenwever had been closely questioned by the officials of the Archbishop of Bremen as to his former doings and as to his intentions in leaving Luebeck and coming to Rotenburg. Of his negotiations with Henry VIII something was known, and a great deal more was suspected; but no hint of his last negotiations with Bonner and Cavendish had been conveyed to the archbishop, to King Christian, or to any of the princes and towns by whose delegates he was about to be examined.

Hoping, probably, that Henry would intercede for him and obtain his release, Wullenwever did not wish to compromise the King of England. He remained silent as to his proceedings at Hamburg, and even on the rack he did not speak of Bonner and Cavendish, but asserted that he had acted on behalf of the Count Palatine Frederic, who pretended a right to the Danish throne.

Henry was less prudent. On hearing of the arrest of Wullenwever, he wrote to the senate and to the Archbishop of Bremen in such violent terms that the latter could not but suspect that there must be very special reasons for his interference. Henry called Wullenwever his beloved friend, declared that he had been arrested against all law and equity, complained that he himself had been badly treated by the archbishop, demanded the release of the prisoner, and threatened reprisals on the persons of all Bremen citizens in England if his request were refused.

This threat could have no great effect on the mind of the archbishop, who was on very bad terms with the burghers over whom he was nominally set. Wullenwever remained a prisoner, and was repeatedly examined by the officials of the archbishop, and by delegates sent by Christian III, by Duke Henry of Brunswick, and by the senate of Luebeck.

But Henry was not disheartened even by so decided a rebuff. Bonner and Cavendish wrote once more to the senate of Bremen, asking them to obtain the release of the prisoner and, like the king, threatening them with reprisals.Henry himself penned a second letter to the archbishop, in which he said again that Wullenwever had not been guilty of any crime, and pretended that his friend, being in prison, was unable to defend himself or to prove his innocence. Christopher had committed a sacrilege, Henry went on, in behaving as he had done; and he was asked to believe that if Wullenwever had really offended against the emperor, Henry, as the great friend of Charles, would punish him most severely. To Henry the prisoner was to be delivered, and, if Christopher declined, signal vengeance was to be taken on his subjects.

The archbishop, exasperated by this arrogant letter, replied that although it professed to be only a friendly representation on behalf of an innocent man, it read rather like a declaration of war. In this matter nothing had been done that was contrary to law or justice, for, as a prince of the empire, the archbishop had full jurisdiction over all persons in his territory. He was ready to justify his acts before the emperor and the electors, to whom Henry might complain if he chose. Should the King of England proceed against citizens of Bremen, Christopher would appeal to the princes of the empire, and sharp retaliatory measures might follow.

Henry and his ministers seem to have understood at last that the archbishop was not to be frightened. The correspondence ceased, and the Bremen citizens were not molested. Bonner and Cavendish, however, tried another way. They addressed a long letter to the King of Denmark, lecturing him about his duties as a Christian, and exhorting him to forgive past offences and not to persecute Wullenwever any longer. This production had no more effect than the preceding letters. The prisoner was kept in close confinement at Rotenburg.

Henry did far more harm than good to the ex-burgomaster. His violence increased the suspicions of Wullenwever's enemies, and the prisoner was more closely questioned as to his dealings with the English ambassadors. At last, on 27 January, having been racked several times, and seeing that no help was likely to come, he confessed all that had passed at Hamburg between him and Bonner and Cavendish. After this he declared in his dungeon that even two kings of England would not be able to save his life.

If the course taken in this matter did no good to Wullenwever, it did much harm to Henry. It had been arranged that after the arrival of Fox and Heath in Saxony, and after the return of the elector from Vienna, the proposals of Henry should be considered by the members of the league of Schmalkalden. While the princes and delegates were sitting, they heard of Wullenwever's arrest and of Henry's outrageous talk. Peter Schwaben, who was present as the ambassador of Christian III, bitterly complained of Henry's dealings with the Luebeck demagogues; and the assembly, impressed by his appeal, decided to let the King of England know that he must no longer oppose the new King of Denmark or assist those who withstood his lawful authority. A few days later, in reply to Henry's proposals for a league, the princes made counter-proposals, which clearly showed how thoroughly they distrusted him. They asked that Henry should accept the Augsburg confession, and that he should give them 100,000 crowns to aid them in defending themselves against the opponents of their faith. In return they offered him a barren title of protector of the league and a promise not to assist his enemies.

Henry was not told the whole truth, for he was allowed to believe that the Wittenberg theologians approved of the divorce and of his marriage with Anne. Even with the facts which were reported to him, however, he was displeased, and in his reply to his ambassadors he refused to be ordered by others as to the faith of his realm, although he declared himself ready to hear what the German theologians might have to say about further reformation. The title of protector of the league he did not immediately accept, but the 100,000 crowns he was willing to deposit for the defence of the Protestant princes and towns.

Shortly afterwards a second set of instructions were forwarded to the ambassadors. In these instructions it is said that Henry 'knoweth not that the Bishop of Rome, the emperor, or any other prince picketh any quarrel with him, and much less war; and although his grace feared some hostility of them, nevertheless, by the death of a woman, all calumnies be extincted.' He asks that, in case any prince shall invade his dominions, the members of the Schmalkaldic League shall furnish him with 500 horse or with ten ships of war at their own cost for four months, and that they shall find him at his expense 2,000 horse and 5,000 foot. Finally, he requires 'that the said confederates will take upon them in all councils hereafter, and everywhere else, to promote and defend the opinion of the reverend fathers, Dr Martyn, Justus Jonas, Cruciger, Pomeran, and Melanchthon, in the cause of his grace's marriage.'

Meanwhile, apart from Henry's foreign policy, the prospects of Anne had not been improving. On the day on which Catherine's death had been reported at court, she had shown the greatest exultation. She had come to hate Catherine most cordially, and rejoiced at the tidings that her detested rival was no more. For, up to this time, every success Anne had gained, every distinction she had obtained, had remained incomplete. She had been proclaimed queen, and heavy penalties had been threatened against those who refused her that title. But Catherine had remained firm, and Henry had not dared to proceed against her to the full extent of his laws. And Anne knew full well that by ninety-nine out of every hundred Englishmen, by nine out of every ten even of her own servants, she herself was secretly regarded as a concubine and usurper, while the prisoner at Kimbolton was considered the lawful wife and queen. Now and then this feeling displayed itself. If wise men were afraid to speak, fools were bolder. We find it related that in July the king's jester in open court called Anne and little Elizabeth opprobrious names. Henry was so angry that Sir Nicholas Carew hid the culprit away; but after a short time the king's wrath subsided, and the jester reappeared.

Fallen as Catherine was from her former greatness, she could not be wholly deprived of the honour due to the daughter of the great Catholic kings, the aunt of the Kaiser, the kinswoman of nearly every royal family in Europe. She was still spoken of with respect; and Christian princes, even when they were politically opposed to her, protested against the manner in which she was treated. Anne, on the contrary, was reminded every day of the lowness of her origin, and Henry himself often taunted her with it. No foreign prince unequivocally recognised her as the lawful Queen of England. The German Protestants, following the advice of their theologians, held that Catherine was Henry's wife. Francis I, the only king who ever expressed a kind of friendship for Anne, acknowledged the pope's authority in the matter of the divorce, and could never be brought absolutely to admit the validity of her marriage. As to his ministers, we have seen how little respect they now showed her.

In these circumstances the death of Catherine seemed at first sight a great gain for the cause of Anne. Now that she was without a rival, it was possible to hope that all the opposition offered to her would die out, and that, having no other queen to revere, people would generally acknowledge her claims. But a very little reflection brought her to a better appreciation of her position. On the day after Catherine's death she held a small council with her brother Rochford and a few of her most tried friends. The precise result of the conference does not appear, but it was remarked that Anne's joy quickly subsided. For the first time, perhaps, she understood why Henry had so ardently desired the death of his wife.

But Anne Boleyn was not a woman to succumb without a struggle. She still had a considerable hold over Henry, who stood in some awe of her intelligence, her energy, and her courage. If she could contrive to help him over the worst of his difficulties, she might regain much of her power, and at least postpone her fall. Now, one of Henry's chief difficulties arose from the persistency with which Mary asserted her rights. By her stubborn resistance to his demands she encouraged her adherents to oppose him, and in case of an insurrection her friends might prove very formidable. Could Mary be brought to yield, the king would be delivered from a serious danger; the one person capable of being put forward as a pretender against him would thereby lose most of her influence.

A few days after Catherine's death Cromwell said to a servant of Chapuis that Charles had no reason to regret an event which would have a good effect on the relations of the empire and England, and that henceforward he would communicate more frequently and more fully with the ambassador. All that was wanted was, that Mary should be persuaded to submit to the king, and in this respect Chapuis would be able to do more than anybody else. Chapuis certainly ought to try to influence her, for by doing so he would not only greatly please the king, but benefit Mary who, if she gave way, would be treated better than she had ever been. These suggestions were, of course, disregarded by the ambassador, and for the moment he rather avoided Cromwell.

This effort having failed, Anne determined to try whether she could not accomplish a task which was beyond the powers of others; believing that if she succeeded Henry would be less eager to abandon her, and might even reward her with as much gratitude as his nature permitted. First of all, she endeavoured to attain her object by means of what seemed to her to be very generous offers. Mary was told through Lady Shelton that if she would act as a dutiful daughter towards the king, Anne would be to her a second mother and strive to obtain for her everything she could desire. And if Mary should afterwards wish to come to court, she would be held excused from bearing Anne's train and would always walk by her side. That is to say, Mary was to take rank before every other lady at court, Anne herself excepted; she was to have all honour shown to her as at the height of her former fortune. Even ladies of the blood royal were obliged occasionally to bear the queen's train, and the princesses were not always entitled to walk at the queen's side. The greatness of the offer shows how much Anne desired to see Mary at her court.

But Anne had misunderstood Mary's character. Her opposition to the divorce and to the subsequent Acts was not due only to her regard for her mother, nor was her resistance after Catherine's death influenced by worldly considerations. So when Lady Shelton implored her with tears to submit to the will of the king, Mary would give no other answer but that she wished to obey her father in everything that was not opposed to her honour and conscience. The acceptance of the new statutes she considered contrary to both. She stood up not only for her mother's fair fame, but for the authority of the pope and the tenets of the Church of Rome.

Instead of promises, threats were now tried. Anne wrote to Lady Shelton that she was not to take any further trouble with that obstinate and undutiful girl. All that Anne had hitherto done had been out of charity and pity, and she was indifferent whether Mary submitted or not. She merely wanted to save Mary before she herself should give birth to a son, as she shortly expected to do. For after the birth of a prince – she well knew – the king would not hesitate to punish Mary, and no mercy would be shown to her. This letter Lady Shelton, as if by chance, dropped in Mary's oratory; and the princess, finding it there, read it and took a copy of it, which she sent to Chapuis. Mary was frightened for a moment, but she did not yield, and a message from Chapuis sustained her courage.

Anne was bitterly disappointed to find that the will she had attempted to bend was as inflexible as her own. She was seen to cry, and was extremely harassed and agitated. Almost her only hope now lay in the pregnancy to which she had alluded in her letter to Lady Shelton. The statement was true; and if she was lucky enough to bear Henry a son, he might in his joy forget everything else and once more return under her sway. But the excitement of the last few days had told upon her health, which constant anxiety had been steadily undermining; and on 29 January – the very day on which her rival and victim was buried – she miscarried in the fourth month of her pregnancy.

Henry had no compassion for Anne in her trouble. He went to her bedside, and gruffly told her that he now saw that God would not give him a son; then, rising to leave, he said harshly that when she recovered he would speak to her. The unhappy woman passionately exclaimed that her miscarriage was not her fault. She had been frightened by the way in which the Duke of Norfolk had told her of the king's fall from his horse. Besides, as her love for the king was far greater than Catherine's had ever been, she could not bear to see him making love to others. This imprudent explanation enraged the king, who did not admit her right to reprove him for his unfaithfulness.

Anne had alluded to a fact of which the whole court had lately become aware. The king was making love to Mistress Jane Seymour, or Seamer, the daughter of Sir John Seamer of Wolfhall in Wiltshire. In a letter to Antoine Perrenot, the son of the lord keeper Granvelle, she was described by her ally and friend Eustache Chapuis. Writing on 18 May 1536, Chapuis says that the emperor, or my lord the chancellor, may wish to hear something of the new friend of the king. He continues:

> She is the sister of a certain Edward Semel, who has been in the service of his majesty [the emperor]; she is of middle height, and nobody thinks that she has much beauty. Her complexion is so whitish that she may be called rather pale. She is a little over twenty-five. You may imagine whether, being an Englishwoman, and having been so long at court, she would not hold it a sin to be still a maid. At which this king will perhaps be rather pleased… for he may marry her on condition that she is a virgin, and when he wants a divorce he will find plenty of witnesses to the contrary. The said Semel is not very intelligent, and is said to be rather haughty. She was formerly in the service of the good queen [Catherine], and seems to bear great goodwill and respect to the princess. I am not sure whether later on the honours heaped on her will not make her change her mind.

Chapuis added a few remarks which cannot be decently translated, and Perrenot, while deciphering the letter, interspersed it with glosses of his own, which, while they do not speak in favour of the propriety of the future cardinal, show that he had no very exalted opinion of Jane's virtue.

The account given by Chapuis to the secretary seems upon the whole to have been correct. If we may judge by her portraits, Jane was indeed very pale, and by no means remarkably handsome. There is nothing in her career which indicates superior intelligence; and although Henry necessarily affected to believe in her virtue, she was no better than the other young women of a coarse and dissolute court.

But she had a very great advantage. Nearly the whole court favoured her, and the most intimate servants of the king instructed her how to humour him. The consequence was that she played her game more skilfully than any of her predecessors, with the exception of Anne, had done. While trying to fascinate Henry, and to be as much as possible in his company, she resisted his wishes, and made a great profession of high principles. That he believed in her sincerity is improbable, his opinion of others being always extremely low. But he was as well pleased with a decent appearance of virtue as with virtue itself, which he had been taught by Catherine to associate with many disagreeable characteristics. Jane's influence, therefore, increased, and the whole party of Anne became seriously alarmed.

The malcontents were highly pleased; but their councils were divided. Those who were nearest the court hoped that, by the aid of Mistress Seymour, they might effect their purpose without having recourse to open rebellion. The other party, on the contrary, thought that their hopes had been too often deceived, and that the safest plan would be to rise in the spring. Chapuis, who had not yet received new instructions, did not wish to commit himself: he favoured neither the one opinion nor the other, but prepared quietly for the flight of Mary and for his own safety in case of a rupture.

Before Anne's miscarriage, a few days after Catherine's death, the king said in strict confidence to one of his most trusted servants, so Chapuis was informed by Lord and Lady Exeter, that he had been driven by sorcery to marry Anne, and that he thought such a marriage could not be valid. God himself clearly showed its invalidity by not granting him male offspring. When Anne recovered from her confinement, Henry continued to treat her with marked coldness. She had been accustomed to follow him wherever he went; now she had to remain at Greenwich while he spent with his courtiers a merry shrovetide in London. The altered demeanour of the king towards Anne was generally remarked, and held to bode no good to her.

Anne's former allies, the French, were now among her most active enemies. As soon as Francis I had received du Bellay's letters, containing a copy of the proposed sentence, he had sent off a courier to Rome with instructions to his ambassadors. They were ordered not to interfere in favour of Henry: whether the sentence against him was issued or not, whether it was severe or mild, whether it deprived him of his kingdom or only laid him under spiritual censures, was all the same to the King of France. The letter reached Rome on the evening of 9 December, and was read by du Bellay with mingled wonder and dismay. The tone of his reply shows how sorry he was that he could not use the influence of Francis on behalf of Henry and Anne.

On the day after the courier arrived at Rome a consistory was held about the English business, and the pope caused an altered draft of the sentence to be read to the cardinals. In sending a copy of this draft to their king du Bellay and Denonville wrote:

> We have followed your orders point by point. The thing appears to everybody to be badly drawn up and full of danger for the future, but it is according to your wishes. We presume you are content that the sentence should be on the one hand so severe and on the other so unjust, that you may be able to make such use of it as your affairs require. If this be so, your intention has been very well fulfilled.

To the Cardinal of Lorraine and the Cardinal of Tournon, du Bellay wrote at greater length, giving them an account of what had passed in the consistory. The pope was extremely irritated on finding that in the opinion of nearly all the cardinals the sentence was too severe, and that they thought he ought not to issue it without first citing Henry to appear and show cause why he should not be excommunicated for having killed Cardinal Fisher. Cardinal Schomberg was in favour of proceeding at once, but he thought the terms of the bull too severe. Schomberg, Contarini, and Gonzaga represented to the pope that times were changed, that the papal power was somewhat less than it had been, and that regard ought to be had to the irritation which such a sentence might produce among foreign nations. This roused the anger of the pope. God, he declared, had placed him above emperor, kings, and princes, and he fully intended to make use of his power. As to the sentence, it was a perfectly proper one; it had been drawn up by men whose fitness for the task was above suspicion. Some cardinal – probably du Bellay – said the emperor and the King of France ought first to be consulted, but the pope answered that he had consulted them long ago. The emperor had replied that, if the pope did his duty, he would show by executing the sentence to the utmost of his ability that he was the true friend and protector of the Holy See.

And the king, to give him his due, after having greatly blamed the abominable misdeeds of the King of England, had promised as much if the emperor kept his word.

Du Bellay was taken aback by this statement, having never heard that any such promise had been made by Francis. But of late he had not been very well informed as to the policy of the king, and, mindful of his instructions, he remained silent.

Schomberg, aided by Campeggio, tried to induce du Bellay to explain the position of the King of France in this matter. Campeggio urged that in issuing the sentence the pope ought not to offend those princes who had some understanding with Henry, especially the most Christian king. It was said that the King of France was a great friend of the King of England, and that they had concluded a treaty of alliance which both kept secret. Schomberg made a more direct effort to compel du Bellay to reveal what he knew. He reminded the consistory of the promptness with which Pope Clement had acted in a moment of difficulty. Some persons had made a show of promoting a reconciliation of Henry with the Church, and had pretended that he was sending a mandate, when in reality astute men were being despatched to enter a protest. Clement, perceiving this, without waiting for the customary forms, had pronounced sentence, deceiving thereby those who had hoped to take him in.

At this very direct attack du Bellay fired up. He first ironically thanked Campeggio for the care with which he watched over the interests of Francis. Then he launched into a long discourse, defending his own action and that of his king. He had begun to speak of the meeting of Marseilles, and was saying that all would have been satisfactorily arranged but for the Bishop of Winchester, when the pope broke in: 'And nevertheless,' he exclaimed, 'that very scoundrel, that accursed man, is even now ambassador with the most Christian king.' Du Bellay went on to say that at Calais Francis had withdrawn from the negotiations about the marriage of Angoulême and Elizabeth, which would have made the young duke the future King of England, because Henry insisted on certain articles in the treaty that might ultimately have brought about some danger of discord between the Holy See and France. 'No,' interrupted the pope, 'your king broke off because the King of England wanted to have the Duke of Angoulême as a hostage. That I know perfectly well.'

The cardinal, according to his own account, replied with no more moderation than was necessary, and he and the pope seem to have had a violent quarrel. At last Cardinal de Cupis, who on that day acted as dean of the college, managed to quiet the pope. Du Bellay, on his part, gave up further opposition, and agreed that the pope might issue the bull without submitting it once more to the college of cardinals.

The matter remained in suspense for a few weeks, for Paul III himself, however incensed against Henry, could not but feel some misgivings as to the effect the bull might produce. No public step, therefore, had been taken when the news of Catherine's death arrived. This suggested to the pope a possibility of new combinations; and as he thoroughly mistrusted du Bellay and du Bellay's friend, Denonville, he sent for the French secretary, Nicolas Raince, and opened his mind to him. He simply wished Francis to offer the hand of his daughter Madeleine to Henry. For the sake of so great a match, Henry might be prepared to discard Anne and to return to communion with Rome. Raince seems to have reported the matter to his friends at the French court, and in subsequent letters we find hints that Francis really took up the matter and felt his ground in England, or at least gave out that he was doing so.

The fact was, Francis now thoroughly understood that it was necessary to make a choice; that if he continued to stand by Henry and Anne he would entirely lose the goodwill of the pope. And as Henry did not offer him any great advantages, the choice was soon made. The death of Catherine only confirmed Francis in his purpose, for Henry, feeling more secure, became much less tractable. The object of the new policy of the French king was to bring about an understanding with the emperor; and he formally undertook to forsake the King of England if Charles would satisfy his demands with regard to Italy. Du Bellay, who was considered too violent and too friendly to Henry and Anne, was recalled from Rome; and after his departure the French agents with the pope, so far from opposing the issuing of the sentence, seem, about the end of March, to have urged the pope publicly to excommunicate the former ally of their master. Francis, having ceased to look for any considerable assistance from Henry, wished to have the sentence published, that Charles might be prevented from concluding an alliance with England.

After the failure of Anne's attempt to subdue Mary, the princess had not been further molested, and in some minor points Cromwell had granted the requests made in her name by Chapuis. Nevertheless, feeling uneasy about her safety, the ambassador went on with his preparations for her flight. But towards the end of February he received a message to the effect that Cromwell desired to have a secret interview with him at St Austin's church. On the 24th Chapuis complied with this request, and the secretary, after complaining of some news he had received from France, began to speak of a closer alliance between Charles and Henry, and urged Chapuis to propose conditions. At first the ambassador was somewhat reticent, but after some time he hinted at four conditions which might form a basis for negotiation. What answer would be given, he inquired, if Charles asked, first, that Henry should submit to the pope and acknowledge the power of the Holy See? secondly, that the Princess Mary should be declared legitimate and reinstated in her former rank? thirdly, that the King of England should furnish help against the Turks? and fourthly, that an offensive and defensive alliance should be concluded between Charles and Henry against everybody who might wrong or attack either. Cromwell quickly replied that as to the two latter points there would be no difficulty whatever; the king wished for such an alliance, and was ready to help to fight the Turk. As to the Lady Mary, this certainly was the proper time to arrange her affairs; and he felt sure it would be done to Charles's satisfaction. The first demand presented the only real difficulty. 'Might not the question,' he suggested, 'be referred to commissioners?' Chapuis met this proposal with an absolute refusal; he would not hear of the matter being referred even to a council called by the emperor. Henry must admit the pope's authority. Afterwards the points in dispute, with the consent of both parties, might be submitted to a council to be called by the pope. Cromwell did not entirely reject these conditions; he only remarked that it would be best to begin the negotiations about some minor matter that would lead in the end to the principal question. He thought the emperor might send Chapuis full powers to treat of a reconciliation and alliance.

The French he continued to condemn in strong terms; and in doing so he used an expression which could not but arrest the attention of the ambassador. He said that the conduct of Francis was resented not only by him and his friends but by the chief of those who were in receipt of French pensions – Norfolk, Suffolk, and Fitzwilliam – even, he added, by the other party and faction. The reference was to Lord Wiltshire; and the obvious intention of Cromwell was to show that he no longer desired to be associated with the adherents of Anne. He ended by asking Chapuis to be of good cheer with regard both to the rights of the Lady Mary and to all other matters still undecided. Let him remember the wonders that had been accomplished since Cromwell had had the direction of the royal affairs.

Chapuis immediately wrote a detailed account of the conversation to his master, and, pointing out the advantages that might be derived from a reconciliation with England, he asked for further instructions and, if a reconciliation was to be effected, for the necessary powers. The direct route to Italy being unsafe, the courier to whom this despatch was entrusted was obliged to take a roundabout way, and, as the roads at that time of the year were bad, his journey lasted no less than five weeks. At last, on 29 March, he overtook the emperor at Gaeta on his way to Rome.

6

Charles V & Anne

On 28 February 1536, Charles V received a packet containing three letters from Chapuis, dated 18 December, 30 December and 9 January. He immediately sent the ambassador new instructions. Chapuis was to take up the proposals for a reconciliation and for a closer alliance which had been made by Henry on 30 December; the pretext being that since the queen was dead it might be unnecessary to adopt further measures with regard to the sentence, or to remit the matter to a council, if only Mary were fairly treated. Henry was to be advised that the best way of dealing with the princess would be to arrange for her some honourable marriage. These instructions were not seriously meant, for the emperor, seeing Henry so obstinate about Anne, thought that a good understanding was in the meantime impossible. But he considered it expedient to seem to be carrying on negotiations. King Francis would hear of them, his insolence would be somewhat checked, and he might even be brought, if he were made sufficiently angry with Henry, to treat with Charles to the advantage of Mary. In any case time would be gained, and when Charles had beaten the French he would be better able to dictate his conditions as to the princess and as to English affairs in general.

The letter written by Chapuis on 24 February changed the emperor's opinion; and on the day on which he received it new and more detailed instructions were sent to the ambassador. They were highly characteristic of the emperor and of his advisers. Charles had been a staunch friend of Catherine, and even after her death he never admitted that the divorce was legal. In this respect he acted in a perfectly honourable manner, postponing his interest to what he considered right and due to his aunt. But, on the other hand, although he believed that Catherine had been poisoned, although he knew that she had been persecuted at Anne's request, he either thought of her wrongs with perfect composure, or concealed his indignation to suit the exigencies of his policy. He himself, as he had already proved, and as he proved still more decisively at a later period, was so ready to plan and order murders, that he may have felt it would be slightly absurd to resent a murder committed by an adversary. His new instructions to Chapuis were, therefore, a model of cool and able statecraft, as statecraft was understood in the sixteenth century.

As to the four points raised by the ambassador, the difficulties of the first did not seem to the emperor to be very great. It related to the sentence of divorce and to the refusal of the annates. If the claims of the princess were respected, the complications connected with the sentence might be avoided; and regarding the annates Charles would do his utmost at the court of Rome to settle the dispute to Henry's satisfaction. Chapuis was to urge that the princess should be expressly declared legitimate, and to point out that this might be done in virtue of the *bona fides parentum*. If Henry would not concede so much, he ought at least to let the matter remain in suspense, and to make no declaration to the contrary. On the other hand, Mary ought to abandon the hostile tone she had adopted, and should not ask the emperor to support her claims by force or to do more than he had done already. The emperor wrote:

> As long as the king lives, the said princess cannot pretend to anything more, nor can we or any other of her relatives proceed much further by asking for other things in her favour. It matters not what the wrong done to her late mother may have been. For she cannot in good conscience insist upon avenging this wrong on her father or consent to its being done by others, even if the life of her mother has been, as is suspected, shortened by foul means. If the sentence about the divorce be executed in order that the king may forsake his concubine, he may marry somebody else, while it is quite clear that from the said concubine he can have no progeny that can hereafter dispute the right of the princess to the succession.

As clear and logical as possible. If at Henry's death the choice of the nation lay between Mary and Elizabeth, the former would be pretty sure to succeed. And as Anne's marriage was invalid, any son she might have would be illegitimate, and Mary would still have a right to the crown. It was, therefore, to the advantage of Mary and indirectly of Charles that her father should retain his mistress, and in the opinion of the emperor this consideration was more important than any other. So we find the son of Juana la Loca preaching filial respect, the murderer of Vogelsberger and so many others inculcating the duty of forgiving all offences.

But Charles thought that Mary might not be able to control her feelings; perhaps, too, he feared that Henry and Anne, to make quite sure, would prefer to poison her. He added, therefore, that if possible a husband should be found for her out of England. The Infante Dom Luis of Portugal – brother of the empress – would be a very suitable match. The concubine and her adherents, said Charles, would be unreasonable if they objected to such a marriage, for the Portuguese were peaceful neighbours. He continued:

> But should the concubine not be satisfied with the proposal either that Mary should be legitimated, or that the matter should be left in suspense – a proposal which, after all, she and all her adherents ought to welcome as a means of escape from the fear and danger in which they now continually are – and should she claim more for her daughter, or for the children she may still have, the negotiation must not for that be broken off. Her ultimate object must be found out. And after you have made to her such observations as you think may serve, you shall say that you will write to us about it, unless indeed the thing be too exorbitant.

Granvelle here added a few words on the draft of the letter to the effect that Chapuis was in this matter to ask for Cromwell's help. He was to communicate the above. If there was anything the concubine or her adherents were not to know, a certain sign would be made. And the sign appears before a paragraph setting forth that if Henry had already decided to discard Anne and to take somebody else, Chapuis was not to offer too much opposition, unless the king wanted to marry a Frenchwoman.

This despatch shows how far Charles was ready to go. For years he had been the bitterest enemy of Anne. Now his ambassador was ordered to treat with her, to negotiate with her a kind of truce, almost an alliance. So strong were the terms of the first draft of the letter that Granvelle, fearing Chapuis might defend Anne even against Henry himself, warned him that this was to be done only under certain conditions.

The explanation of all these concessions was indicated in the last two points noted in the instructions. Charles wanted aid against the Turk, and he wanted an alliance against Francis; at least, Henry was to defend the Low Countries or to give a good sum of money for the war. The emperor would have found it quite compatible with his religion to pocket the proceeds of the sale of the abbey lands; and had Anne been able to obtain for him so great a favour, he would have thanked her for it by smoothing over her difficulties.

The courier who carried this reply did not travel more rapidly than the one who had brought the letter of Chapuis. The consequence was that the ambassador did not receive his new instructions before 15 April. In the meantime a good deal had happened to change the situation.

The influence of Jane Seymour had greatly increased. By the end of February her brother Edward Seymour had been made a gentleman of the king's privy chamber. In the middle of March, when Jane was with the court at Greenwich, Henry sent her from London a letter and a purse full of sovereigns. This gave her an opportunity of making a fine show of virtue. She took the king's letter, kissed it in token of respect and devotion, but returned it unopened; then, falling on her knees, she charged the gentleman who had brought it to do the same to the king, and to beseech him in her name to remember that she was a gentlewoman sprung from a good and honourable stock, free from any taint whatever. She had no greater treasure in this world than her honour; not even fear of death would make her forget it. She would not take the purse, but said that if the king wanted to make her a present, let it be when God should send her some good and honest husband. The gentleman, who seems to have been a friend of Jane, returned to Henry with the purse and the letter, and delivered the lady's message. The king was by no means displeased; the next time he saw her he greatly praised the modest and prudent answer she had sent him. She had acted most virtuously, he said; and to give her full proof that the love he bore her was honest, henceforward he would not speak to her except in the presence of some of her relatives. That the good king might suffer no loss by his scrupulous delicacy, Cromwell had to give up a room he occupied in the palace. In this room, which had the advantage of being accessible by a secret passage, Sir Edward Seymour and his wife were lodged, and there Jane received her lover.

Henry was probably not aware that the highly moral speeches of Jane were not even of her own invention, but that she was taught by his attendants how to behave. Sir Nicholas Carew, Sir Thomas Eliot and other intimate servants of the king warned her not to yield to Henry unless he married her, and Jane was wise enough to follow their advice. At a given moment, they further urged, she was to tell the king that the whole nation held his marriage with Anne in abomination, and that nobody considered it valid. All around there were to be people who would confirm what she said, if the king ordered them on their allegiance to tell him the truth. For this purpose the help of Chapuis was desired; and the Marchioness of Exeter, who kept the ambassador well informed of all that went on at court, sent him a message on 1 April imploring him to lend his aid.

Chapuis, who had not yet received his new instructions, felt rather inclined to grant the request of Lady Exeter. Since the meeting at Austin friars Cromwell had shown himself more and more friendly to the imperial ambassador and to the imperial party. In the beginning of March he happened to speak to Doctor de Lasco, whom Henry wanted to place with Mary; and the doctor observed that when Cromwell pronounced the princess's name he raised his cap – a mark of respect with which he had never before honoured her. A little cross of gold which Catherine from her deathbed had sent to Mary, had been taken away by the royal officials. A few days after speaking to de Lasco, Cromwell had it sent back to the princess.

But Cromwell did more than all this. In the reply which the English ambassadors at the Saxon court were to make to the Schmalkaldic princes, there was, as we have seen, a paragraph requiring the league to defend the opinion of Luther, Melanchthon and Pomeranus in the matter of the divorce. This paragraph the ambassadors were obliged to suppress, for they knew that the Lutheran theologians had maintained, and continued to maintain, that the marriage with Catherine was valid. At first the royal ministers tried to keep the matter secret; but as it soon began to be talked about, the opinion of the Lutheran divines was laid before a number of bishops and doctors that they might draw up a fitting answer. This was an excellent opportunity for those among them who were adverse to further innovation; and the opportunity was not lost. Members of the reforming party found themselves in a very unpleasant position, and the result of the conference was decidedly unfavourable to Protestantism. Cranmer was unable to restore the credit of his adherents, for he himself was in disgrace with the king. At the very time when Henry wished to be reconciled to Charles, the archbishop had chosen to preach most violently against what he called the usurpations of the imperial power, the supremacy of which he angrily denied.

Seeing the tendency of events, Cromwell apparently began to think in earnest of the possibility of a reconciliation with Rome. The *malleus monachorum*, as he has been called, was heard to protest against the way in which the abbeys were despoiled. He took the side of the conservative churchmen against those who had been hitherto considered Anne's principal supporters; and he did so with a boldness and energy which offended both the vacillating king and Anne. About the end of March the court was full of rumours regarding a serious quarrel between Anne and the secretary.

At a dinner given by Chapuis to the Marquis of Exeter, Lady Kildare, and Lord Montague, the latter told the ambassador of the ill feeling between Cromwell and Anne, and mentioned a report that Henry was bent on a new marriage. Shortly afterwards Chapuis had an interview with Cromwell, to whom he bluntly spoke of what he had heard. If it were true, he said, the secretary ought to prepare for the coming struggle better than Wolsey had done. Did the king really wish to make another marriage, it would be a very good thing, as all his difficulties might then be overcome. Cromwell demurely replied that if the fate of Wolsey overtook him, he would try to bear it patiently. He had been no promoter of the marriage with Anne; he had only found the means by which it could be accomplished when the king vehemently desired it. As to a new marriage, the king in former days had certainly rather loved the fair sex, but Cromwell thought that henceforward he would live more chastely and not change again. But he said this in a way which convinced Chapuis that he meant the contrary; as he spoke, he put his hand before his face to conceal a smile. One thing he assured Chapuis of; if the king re-married, he would not choose his bride in France. During the whole interview Cromwell was most friendly; and when they were about to part, he begged Chapuis to accept a very fine horse as a gift from him.

After this conversation Chapuis felt pretty sure that Cromwell would no longer maintain the cause of Anne. The intrigue which had been proposed by Lady Exeter seemed, therefore, to have every chance of success; and the ambassador considered whether he ought not to become the chief mover in the attempt to drive 'the concubine' from the throne. He saw, however, that the interests of Mary might be imperilled if Henry were free to marry again. Accordingly, before deciding finally, he wrote once more to Mary, and, placing the two sides of the question before her, asked to be informed what her wishes were. As he had expected, she immediately replied that she did not care how her own interests might be affected, if her father could be saved from the sinful life he was leading. She wished Chapuis to do as Lady Exeter had desired, and hoped he would succeed. This decided the ambassador's course. During the following days he had several interviews with Cromwell and with the leading conspirators, and some arrangements had been made when the despatches from Charles arrived.

On receipt of the emperor's letters Chapuis sat down to decipher them at once. As they were rather long he had to work until late at night, but he made a short abstract of such points as he was to communicate, and early next morning he went to Cromwell to request that he might have an audience of the king. The secretary, on hearing what Chapuis had to say, was so pleased that he would have liked to open negotiations without delay. But it was Easter Sunday, and Henry, who always shrank from forming a definite judgment, was glad to have a pretext for putting off the audience. Cromwell had to reply that the ambassador would be received on Tuesday the 18th.

The news that Charles was disposed to be on good terms again with Henry was not kept a strict secret. A good many of the courtiers heard of it, while Anne and her nearest kinsfolk and friends seem to have been more particularly informed as to the proposed articles. Consequently, when Chapuis arrived on Tuesday morning at

Greenwich Palace, he was welcomed by a throng of joyous courtiers, Lord Rochford, Anne's brother, being foremost among them. With Rochford the ambassador had a most friendly conversation, the young lord making loud protestations of his desire for an alliance between England and the emperor. Even then, however, as Chapuis remarked, he spoke as a strong Lutheran which, of course, was not to the taste of the imperial minister.

After a short while Cromwell went to greet Chapuis, and to ask him in Henry's name whether he would not see the queen and kiss hands. The king would be pleased if he did so, but left him entirely free. Chapuis cleverly answered that it might be better to wait until he had conferred with the king about the new proposals; and with this opinion Cromwell agreed. Henry also, when the secretary reported to him what Chapuis had said, declared himself satisfied.

The truth is, if Chapuis had thought that he would have gratified the king and advanced the interests of his master by allowing himself to be presented to Anne as queen, he would gladly have gone. As he wrote to Granvelle, he would have been ready, had Henry been tractable, to offer, not a pair of candles, but a hundred, on the altar either of the devil or of the she-devil. But he had been warned that she was in disgrace, and that it would be of no use to pay his court to her.

Coming out of his apartment to go to mass, Henry plainly showed that the refusal of Chapuis had not displeased him. He was most gracious to the ambassador. After this the king went on, and Rochford again placed himself by the side of Chapuis to accompany him to the chapel. There was a great rush after them, for as Anne was also going to mass she and Chapuis would be brought face to face; and the host of idle courtiers were curious to see how they would behave to each other. Chapuis was placed close to the door by which Anne was to enter, probably in order that he might be quite near her. It had not been observed that after the opening of the door he would be concealed behind it. Anne, however, knowing that he was there, turned round as she passed. He made her a deep bow, and she responded with as deep and gracious a salute. Then she swept on to her place at the king's side. A good many people who had hoped that Chapuis would be rude to his former enemy were grievously vexed, and Mary herself was astonished when she heard that the ambassador of the emperor had bowed to 'that woman'.

After mass Henry went to Anne's rooms, where he was accustomed to dine. The foreign ambassadors and most of the courtiers followed him, but Chapuis – with Rochford always at his side – dined with the principal noblemen in the chamber of presence. Anne seems to have been disappointed that Chapuis did not attend her to her apartments, for she asked the king why he had not come with the other ambassadors. Henry, annoyed by the question, answered that Chapuis had good reasons for staying away. Nevertheless, Anne was resolved to throw in her lot with the imperial faction; and after dinner she spoke strongly against Francis. 'It was a great shame,' she said, 'that the King of France treated his uncle the Duke of Savoy so badly, and intended to invade Milan in order to prevent further action against the Turks. It seems,' she exclaimed, alluding to the infamous disease of Francis, 'that the King of France, tired of life on account of his illness, wants to shorten his days by going to war.' These remarks were of course repeated, and they were meant to show that there was an open rupture between her and her former friends.

In the afternoon Henry left Anne's rooms, and taking the ambassador into the recess of a window, prepared to hear his communication. When Chapuis had submitted his proposals, Henry broke out into the most extravagant talk, declaring that he would make no concessions, and boasting in a preposterous way about his greatness and power, and about the benefits he had heaped upon Charles. Chapuis, although irritated by this bragging, allowed the king to go on, that he might have his fill of vainglory and slowly quiet down. But Henry would not quiet down; he refused to listen to reason, and insisted, among other things, that Charles should acknowledge himself to have been altogether in the wrong, and should either have the papal sentence quashed or declare that it had been obtained against justice by threats.

By and by, the king called Cromwell and the Lord Chancellor Audeley into the recess, and asked Chapuis to repeat his message to them. When they had heard it, the ambassador retired and began to speak with Sir Edward Seymour, keeping, however, a watchful eye on the little group at the window. He could soon perceive that there was an acrimonious dispute between the king and Cromwell. After a protracted discussion the secretary called out that he was so thirsty he could not bear it any longer, and, snorting and puffing with anger, he left the king and Audeley, and went to sit on a chest where Henry could not see him.

After a while Henry left the chancellor; and Chapuis, perceiving that for the moment nothing more could be done, made ready to depart. Henry was a little more gracious when the ambassador came to take his leave, but he made no concessions. Chapuis was accompanied by many of the courtiers to the gates, where he mounted his horse. They were rather crestfallen, and some of the councillors said plainly that they were very sorry for what had happened. On the road Chapuis was overtaken by Cromwell, who was also riding back to London; and the secretary did not hide his vexation at the obstinacy and folly of the king. He was in a state of such excitement that when he arrived at his lodgings at Roll's house he had to take to his bed, where he remained for several days.

Antoine de Castelnau, Bishop of Tarbes, the resident French ambassador, soon heard of the negotiations opened by Chapuis; so, curious to know what had been the result, he went on the following day to Greenwich. He saw the Duke of Norfolk, who assured him that, whatever the emperor might offer or propose, the king would not withdraw from the alliance with Francis. Afterwards Castelnau was received by the king, who complained that Francis did not show him sufficient respect, and that a special envoy who should have been sent to him long ago had not yet arrived. The bishop tried to soothe his anger, and at last the king told him about the mission of Chapuis. The four propositions of the imperial ambassador had now swollen into five, besides curiously altering their nature. The first referred to the day when Charles V would enter Rome. Secondly, Charles asked Henry to intercede with the French king in favour of the Duke of Savoy. Thirdly, fearing that Francis might invade Milan, Charles begged Henry to help him if he were so attacked. Fourthly, Henry was entreated to forget all that had passed between him and the emperor on account of Catherine, and to renew the old treaties of friendship and confederation. The fifth proposition set forth a demand for aid against the Turk. Henry pretended that as to Savoy he had replied in a manner quite favourable to Francis. He warned the bishop that Charles was raising a large army with which to repel the French, and advised the king not to advance any further, but to fortify the conquests he had made, and to await the emperor's attack.

Castelnau thanked Henry for the friendly feeling he had exhibited, and immediately after his return to London wrote an account of the audience to his master. He added that at this moment Henry seemed most favourably inclined.

Anne's position was now a very strange one. After years of unrelenting hostility the emperor had proposed the terms of a truce which appeared likely, as the death of Catherine had appeared likely, to be of great advantage to her. If she could have had her way, the offers of Charles would have been accepted; and had she been willing to give up Protestantism, she might then have persuaded Henry to submit to the pope, who would have given absolution to both of them and recognised the validity of their marriage from the time of Catherine's death. But it was too late to hope for these great results. New influences were at work – some of them of Anne's own creation – over which she had no control, and which brought her to the scaffold.

When Henry obstinately refused to submit to the pope, it was not only his vanity which was at play; he was impelled also by greed and by fear of rebellion. By an act of parliament passed in March a good many abbeys had been dissolved, and their lands vested in the king. His coffers had thus been filled, and he had been enabled to meet the expenses of government and of an extravagant court without exasperating his people by odious taxes. Submission to Rome meant for him the loss of this agreeable and plentiful source of income; it meant retrenchment and economy – a prospect which had no attractions for him. But it meant even more. A good part of the abbey lands seized by the king's officers had been granted away to his servants and courtiers, or to the lords and gentry in the neighbourhood of the confiscated estates. These favoured persons, and others who expected similar bounties, had a direct interest in opposing a reconciliation with the Holy See, which might have endangered the peaceful possession of what they held and cut off all hope of new spoliation. As long as Henry was firmly resolved not to return to communion with Rome, it may have been excellent policy to give away abbey lands, but his generosity at the expense of the church made it very difficult for him to alter his course.

Among those to whom large grants had been made were the Duke of Norfolk, the Duke of Suffolk, and several other recipients of French pensions. They became the leaders of the party opposed to submission to the pope; and as Cromwell had begun to speak against the destruction of the abbeys, and had resisted further grants, they looked upon him as their great enemy. During the illness which kept Cromwell at Roll's house, Norfolk ruled supreme at the council board, and he employed his time very well. The official party without their chief presented but a poor front; they could not thwart so powerful a peer. The object of Norfolk now was to throw Henry into the arms of Francis, to make reconciliation with Charles and with the Holy See impossible, and to displace the imperialist first secretary. He succeeded so far that on the 22nd Henry summoned Castelnau to his presence, and asked him to go to France and explain the whole position to Francis, and to obtain the speedy conclusion of a treaty of alliance. As Henry seemed ready to grant terms most advantageous to Francis, the bishop consented, and returned to London to prepare for his journey.

Henry was not, however, without misgivings. Had he, by rejecting the proposals transmitted by Chapuis, definitively closed the door to a reconciliation with the emperor? That would be extremely awkward, for if it were made known the French would become as arrogant as ever. He was already half sorry for what he had done. Sending for de Lasco, about whose future service with Mary he pretended that he wanted to speak, he closely questioned the doctor as to the way in which Chapuis had talked since his audience at Greenwich. He was evidently afraid of the anger of the ambassador.

It was in this state of mind that Cromwell found his royal master when after his brief illness he returned to court. The secretary had had time to review quietly the whole situation, and he had arrived at the conclusion that vigorous action on his part had become inevitable. By opposing the further destruction of abbeys, by stoutly advocating the imperial alliance and the concessions necessary to obtain it, he had kindled the anger of Henry, of the greedy courtiers, and of the French faction. His position was threatened, Norfolk was gaining on him, and by some means or other he must strengthen his hold over the king. It would be necessary to teach Henry that he could not afford to dispense with his secretary's services. He would have to be confronted by some difficulty which he could hope to dispose of only with the aid of the powerful and complicated organisation over which Cromwell presided.

At this moment there was a difficulty which, if brought to a crisis, might be made to serve. Henry had been so well worked upon by Jane Seymour and her friends that he ardently wished to be rid of a woman with whom he was no longer in love, and who could not bear him the son he desired. He had already on several occasions spoken of his marriage with Anne as invalid, and of his intention to proceed with another divorce. He had assured Jane Seymour that his love for her was honourable, and had clearly shown that he intended to marry her. But, as usual, he had not courage to strike the blow with his own hand; he was waiting for some one to take the responsibility of the deed.

Of course Cromwell might have helped to obtain a divorce; but he saw that it would be neither in his own nor in the king's interest to proceed in this manner. To have applied for a divorce would have been to proclaim to the world that Henry, on entering the holy bonds of matrimony, was careless whether there were impediments or not; it would have been to raise a very strong suspicion that the scruples of conscience he had pleaded the first time, were courtly enough to reappear whenever he wanted to be rid of a wife. Henry's reputation would have greatly suffered, and as he knew this himself, although he chafed at his fetters, he dared not cast them off. A second reason – which more especially affected Cromwell – was that Anne, if she were simply divorced, would still remain Marchioness of Pembroke, with a very considerable fortune, and with some devoted friends. Rochford had gained experience, and showed no little ability, and he, acting with his sister, might form a party which would be most hostile to the secretary.

Besides, a divorce could have been secured by Norfolk as easily as by Cromwell. There would really have been no difficulty at all. Cranmer would not have dreamt of disobeying the royal commands; he did in fact pronounce the marriage to be void. Of the other bishops one half were bitterly opposed to Anne, while most of those whose promotion she had aided were supple courtiers who would do the king's bidding. Indeed, we hear of some zealous servant, who, perceiving what was wanted, went on 27 April to consult Stokesley, the Bishop of London, as to whether the marriage between the king and Anne was valid or not. Stokesley, although he hated Anne and the Boleyns, was too cautious to offer an opinion. He said that he would reply to such a question only if it were put by the king himself; and he added that, should the king intend to ask him, he would like to know beforehand the kind of answer that was desired.

For all these reasons it was necessary that Anne should be got rid of in a quicker and more violent way. Difficulties and dangers were to be invented, that Cromwell might save the king from them. Anne was to be found guilty of such heinous offences that she would have no opportunity of avenging her wrongs. Her friends were to be involved in her fall, and the event was to be associated with horrors that would strike the imagination of the king and withdraw the attention of the public from the intrigue at the bottom of the scheme. Calamity was to be brought upon her, too, in a way that would satisfy the hatred with which she was regarded by the nation, and take the ground away under the feet of the conspirators. Thus Cromwell, as he afterwards told Chapuis, resolved to plot for the ruin of Anne.

7

The Arrest

Whether Henry was at once informed that Anne was to be killed is not certain. Probably he was only told by Cromwell that he was menaced by grave dangers, and that it would be necessary to appoint commissioners to hold special sessions at which offenders against him might be tried. On 24 April, in accordance with these representations, the king signed a commission by which the Lord Chancellor Audeley, the Dukes of Norfolk and Suffolk, the Earl of Oxford, lord high chamberlain, the Earl of Westmoreland, the Earl of Wiltshire, lord privy seal, the Earl of Sussex, Lord Sandys, chamberlain of the household, Sir Thomas Cromwell, chief secretary, Sir William Fitzwilliam, treasurer, Sir William Paulet, comptroller of the household, and the nine judges or any four or more of them were empowered to make inquiry as to every kind of treason, by whomsoever committed, and to hold a special session to try the offenders. That this was virtually a death-warrant for Anne, Henry must have known, or at least suspected; but his conscience remained quiet: the deed would be done by others.

The commission was not made public; nor was it communicated to the persons to whom it was addressed. That would have been contrary to all the traditions of the Tudor service. It was kept strictly secret; and only a few chosen instruments were to be employed until the case should be sufficiently prepared. To make out a case against Anne was now the great object of Cromwell, and he began his task with characteristic energy.

The tacit understanding between Henry and Cromwell which led to the signing of the commission restored the secretary to his former influence. When, therefore, the Bishop of Tarbes, ready to leave for

France, repaired to court on 25 April, and asked for the articles he was to submit to his master, he found that they had not been drawn up; and he was kept the whole day at Greenwich, the council sitting and debating until late at night. Although Henry, acting on Cromwell's advice, treated the French coldly, he was not prepared to conciliate the emperor, as he showed clearly enough in a despatch sent at this time to Richard Pate, the English ambassador at the court of Charles V. In giving directions for the composition of this despatch – for it was evidently in substance the work of the king – Henry seems to have resolved to have once more what Chapuis had called, a week before, 'his fill of glory'. He asserted that through his influence Charles had been made King of Spain and Emperor; he rejected and complained of all the conditions Charles had proposed for a reconciliation; he protested that he would not be dictated to; and finally, in a ciphered paragraph at the end, he instructed Pate to ascertain the most favourable terms the emperor might be brought to offer. It was an extremely foolish letter, but Cromwell allowed it to pass, well knowing that a complete change in the state of affairs would shortly render it inoperative. In return for this concession to the king's vanity, he was allowed to add to the articles agreed upon with Castelnau certain demands which, as he knew, Francis would never grant. The consequence was that when the bishop, already somewhat angry at the delay, returned to court on the 27th and heard what was proposed, he indignantly refused to go to France on such an errand. For the moment there was no further danger of a closer alliance with Francis.

Cromwell was thus in a position to devote himself to the work of collecting evidence against Anne. The old stories about her ante nuptial misconduct would not of course suffice. Even with regard to irregularities of which she had been accused after marriage there was a difficulty; for by the statute passed in the autumn of 1534 any statement capable of being interpreted as a slander upon the king's issue might be accounted treason, so that people were rather loath to repeat what they might have heard to Anne's discredit. Cromwell decided, therefore, to have her movements watched closely, in the hope that she might be caught in some imprudence. As most of her servants were secretly her enemies, he did not doubt that some of them would gladly give information against her, if they could do so without risking their own lives.

On the 23rd there had been an election to a place in the Order of the Garter, rendered vacant by the death of Lord Abergavenny. Sir Nicholas Carew and Lord Rochford had been candidates for it, and in ordinary circumstances the brother-in-law of the king would certainly have carried the day. But it was Sir Nicholas, Anne's open enemy, who had been elected. This incident, although insignificant in itself, was of great service to Cromwell, for those who disliked Anne began to think that it could not be very dangerous to speak against her, when she had not influence enough even to obtain a favour for her brother. On the day after the election her opponents sent a triumphant and cheering message to Mary.

It seems to have been Anne's own imprudence which gave Cromwell his first clue. She was exceedingly vain; and, like her daughter Elizabeth, who inherited many of the qualities of her strange character, she delighted in the admiration of men, and fancied that every man who saw her was fascinated by her charms. Her courtiers soon found out that the surest road to her favour was either to tell her that other men were in love with her, or to pretend that they were in love with her themselves. She was extremely coarse, and lived at a most dissolute court; so that the flattery she asked for was offered in no very modest terms. Lately, her health had been giving way, and her mirror had been reminding her that she was getting rather old and losing her good looks. This caused her to crave more than ever for adulation; and her increased coquetry gave rise to scandalous stories, and provided Cromwell with the kind of charges he wanted. On 29 April, at Greenwich, Anne found a certain Mark Smeton, a groom of the chamber to Henry, and a player on the lute, standing in the bow of the window of her chamber of presence. She went up to him, and, according to her own statement, asked him why he was so sad. Smeton replied it was no matter; and she then said, 'You may not look to have me speak to you as I should to a nobleman, because you be an inferior person.' 'No, no,' Smeton replied, 'a look sufficeth me, and so fare-you-well.'

The conversation seems to have been overheard, and to have been reported by Cromwell's spies. Smeton's manner, or that of Anne, had excited suspicion; and when, on the following day, the unhappy musician took his way to London, he was arrested at Stepney and rigorously examined. It is not known how much Smeton confessed at this first examination. He may not have admitted that he had committed adultery with Anne; but he was no hero, and fear of the rack or the hope of pardon probably led him to make statements by which she was seriously compromised and by which other persons were implicated. He was kept in close confinement at a house in Stepney, but his arrest and examination were not immediately made known, for Cromwell wanted further evidence before striking the blow.

Among the friends of Anne there was a young courtier named Sir Francis Weston, the son of Sir Richard Weston, under-treasurer of the exchequer. He had first been a royal page, but had risen to the rank of groom of the privy chamber, and was now one of the gentlemen of it. For the last eight years, by reason of his office, he had resided constantly at court, and he had obtained a good many grants and pensions. In May 1530, he had married Anne, the daughter and heiress of Sir Christopher Pykering; and having thus become a man of considerable property, he was created, at the coronation of Anne, a knight of the Bath.

Another of Anne's friends was Henry Noreys, also a gentleman of the king's chamber, and the keeper of his privy purse. Noreys had been for many years a favourite attendant of Henry. He had at once sided with Anne when she had begun her struggle; and he had been among the foremost of those who had worked the ruin of Wolsey. Ever since the death of the cardinal he had belonged to the little group of personal adherents of the Boleyns. He had married a daughter of Lord Dacres of the South; but having been for some time a widower it had occurred to him that he would please both Henry and Anne if he took as his second wife pretty Margaret Shelton, who, although she had lost her hold on Henry's caprice, had remained at court. So a marriage had been arranged between him and Mistress Margaret. But of late he had become somewhat cold, and Anne attributed his estrangement to jealousy, for she had observed that Sir Francis Weston had been paying rather marked attentions to her cousin. Accordingly, on 23 April she had some private talk with Sir Francis, and upbraided him for making love to Margaret and for not loving his wife. The young man, knowing how great was her appetite for flattery, answered that he loved some one in her house more than either his wife or Margaret Shelton. Anne eagerly asked who it was, and he replied, 'It is yourself.' She affected to be angry, and rebuked him for his boldness; but the reprimand cannot have been very terrible, for Weston continued his talk, and told her that Noreys also came to her chamber more for her sake than for that of Madge, as Margaret Shelton was called.

Finding all this very interesting, Anne took occasion to speak to Noreys, hoping perhaps that he would gratify her with the same kind of compliments as those which had been paid to her by Weston. She asked him why he did not marry her cousin, to which he replied evasively that he would wait for some time. Displeased by this cautious answer, Anne said he was waiting for dead men's shoes, for if aught came to the king but good, he would look to have her. Noreys, being older and more experienced than Weston, understood how dangerous a game he was being made to play. He strongly protested that he dared not lift his eyes so high; if he had any such thoughts, he would his head were cut off. Anne then taunted him with what Weston had told her. She could undo him if she would, she said. About this they seem to have had some words, Noreys being evidently afraid that he might be drawn into a perilous position. Perhaps Anne herself began to feel uneasy, for she ended the conversation by asking Noreys to contradict any rumours against her honour. This he consented to do, and on Sunday, the last day of April, he told Anne's almoner that he would swear for the queen that she was a good woman. Cromwell apparently heard of this conversation, and concluded that the time had almost come for making the case public. Henry was informed of what was about to be done, that he might be ready to play his part.

The following day being May Day, a tournament was held at Greenwich, Henry Noreys and Lord Rochford being among the challengers. The king and Anne were present, and seemed to be still on tolerable terms. When the tilting was over, Henry bade Anne farewell, and, as had lately become his custom, rode off towards London. On the way he called Noreys to his side, and telling him he was suspected of having committed adultery with the queen, urged him to make full confession. Although the king held out hopes of pardon, Noreys refused to say anything against Anne, and protested that his relations with her had been perfectly innocent. Henry then rode away, and Noreys was immediately arrested, and kept, like Smeton, a close prisoner. He was taken to the Tower by Sir William

Fitzwilliam, who, it was afterwards asserted, tried hard to persuade him to confess that he was guilty. Whether, as was further stated, Noreys said anything that compromised Anne is not known, but he certainly did not confess that he had committed adultery with her. Having left him at the Tower – to which Smeton had been brought about the same time – Sir William Fitzwilliam went to Greenwich, where the commissioners were to examine Anne herself.

That evening nothing further was done. Anne was still treated with the outward respect due to a queen, but she knew that her enemies were working against her, and that she was threatened by the greatest dangers. At ten o'clock at night she heard that Smeton was confined in the Tower, and shortly afterwards it was reported to her that Noreys had been sent there too. Combining these facts with Henry's growing coldness to herself, and his increasing affection for Jane Seymour, Anne began to fear that she would have to take the same way. She was absolutely without means of defence. Henry had gone to Westminster to be out of the way, and she could not bring her personal influence to bear on him. The few friends she had were equally out of reach, most of them having gone with the king to London; so she could do nothing but await her doom. Even flight was impossible, for had she been able to leave the palace and to go on board a ship to elude the vigilance of the searchers and to cross the sea she would not have been safe. Neither Charles nor Francis would have afforded her an asylum; her flight would have been taken as a clear proof of guilt, and she would have been given up in accordance with the treaties which forbade the various sovereigns to shelter one another's traitors.

So passed the night. On the following morning Anne received a message requesting her to appear before the council. She obeyed, and was then told of the powers given to the royal commissioners. She was also informed that she was suspected of having committed adultery with three different persons – Smeton, Noreys, and a third whose name does not appear – and that the two former had already confessed the crime. Her remonstrances and protestations had no effect. She subsequently described the behaviour of the commissioners as generally rude. The Duke of Norfolk, who presided, would not listen to her defence; Sir William Fitzwilliam seemed the whole time to be absent in mind; Sir William Paulet alone treated her with courtesy.

At the end of the interrogation, the royal commissioners ordered Anne to be arrested, and she was kept in her apartment until the tide would serve to take her to the Tower. At two o'clock her barge was in readiness, and in broad daylight, exposed to the gaze of the populace who had assembled on the banks or in boats and barges, she was carried along the river to the traitors' gate. She was accompanied by the Duke of Norfolk, Lord Oxford, and Lord Sandys, with a detachment of the guard.

Lord Rochford had already been caught in the toils which had been woven for Anne's destruction. He was an able and energetic man, strongly attached to his sister; and it was foreseen that in so dreadful an emergency he would, if left at large, do everything in his power to save her. So he was arrested towards noon at Westminster, and taken to the Tower. Anne's friends were closely watched, but it was not thought necessary to interfere with the liberty of Lord Wiltshire. He was a mean egotist and coward, and from motives of prudence had always disapproved of his daughter's bold and violent courses. There was, therefore, no reason to fear that he would try to defend her.

At the Tower Anne was received by Sir William Kingston, the constable, of whom Chapuis had reported that he was wholly devoted to Catherine and Mary. To his keeping she was handed over by the commissioners. Up to this moment she seems to have maintained an appearance of firmness; but when the gates had shut behind the departing councillors, when she found herself surrounded by the gloomy walls of the Tower, in the custody of the constable, her courage gave way. She realised the full horror of her situation, and as Kingston beckoned to her to proceed, fearful visions of loathsome prison cells rose before her mind. She tremblingly asked Kingston whether he was leading her to a dungeon. He reassured her, saying that she was to go to the lodging she had occupied before her coronation. This somewhat relieved her distress. 'It is too good for me,' she exclaimed. But, the tension of the last hour having been too much for her shattered nerves, she fell on her knees and burst into hysterical fits of laughter and weeping. When she calmed down she was taken to her apartment, where four gentlewomen under the superintendence of Lady Kingston had been deputed to wait on her. Suspecting what had happened to her brother, she made a few anxious inquiries about him, and Kingston, who seems to have felt some pity for her, merely answered that he had left Lord Rochford that morning at Whitehall. She asked that the eucharist might be exposed in a closet near her room, that she might pray for mercy; and then she began to assert her innocence of the crimes with which she was charged. But these were matters to which Kingston would not listen, and he went away, leaving her to the care of her female gaolers.

The news of Anne's arrest and imprisonment ran like wildfire through the city. It was known that she was accused of having committed adultery with Noreys, or with Noreys and Smeton, and that Lord Rochford and others were somehow involved in the case, but as yet nothing was heard of the charge of incest. Rochford was said to have been arrested for having connived at his sister's evil deeds.

The fate which had overtaken Anne excited little sympathy. Even among the Protestants, who formed at this time in England but a small class, there were some who disliked her. The great majority of the people, detesting the changes of recent years, accused her and her family of having plunged England into danger, strife, and misery in order to satisfy their own ambition and greed. The difficulties abroad and the consequent slackness of trade, the severity of the new laws and the rigour with which they were enforced, were held to be due altogether to Anne's ascendancy; and it was expected that with her downfall there would be a total change of policy, which would place England once more in a secure and prosperous condition.

But there was a man whom the tidings filled with dismay. For some months Cranmer had been ill at ease. The ultra reformers, Anne's friends, had not been favoured since her influence had begun to decay; and the archbishop, who relied chiefly on them, had found himself under a cloud. In the country he received a letter from Cromwell, informing him of the arrest of Anne and of the reasons for it, and ordering him to proceed to Lambeth, there to await the king's pleasure, but not to present himself at court. He obeyed with a heavy heart, for such an order from the secretary boded no good, and Cranmer was not the man to face danger calmly. Next morning, at Lambeth, he wrote a letter to the king, beseeching him not to visit the faults which might be found in the queen on the Church she had helped to build up.

The archbishop had just finished writing when he received a message to appear before the council at Westminster. Such a message at such a time seemed even more ominous than Cromwell's letter, but it was peremptory, and had to be obeyed. Cranmer took his barge, crossed the river, and went to the Star Chamber, where he found the Lord Chancellor Audley, the Earls of Oxford and Sussex, and Lord Sandys. By the terms of the commission of 24 April they formed a quorum; and it is probable that they subjected Cranmer to an examination. But he seems to have been either unable or unwilling to furnish fresh evidence against Anne. The commissioners acquainted him with the proof which they had, or pretended to have, of her guilt; and the primate, cowed by the manner in which he was treated, declared himself satisfied with it. He returned to Lambeth, and there added a postscript to his letter, saying he was exceedingly sorry such things could be proved against the queen.

After this, of course, Cranmer made no attempt to help his former patron. Nor do we hear that her friends at court dared in any way to interfere. The only person who tried to be of service to her was a poor lawyer of Gray's Inn, one Roland Buckley, the brother of a friend of Noreys, Sir Richard Buckley, knight chamberlain of North Wales. As soon as Roland heard of the arrest of Anne and Noreys, he wrote to Sir Richard, who was in favour with the king, beseeching him to come to court and to intercede on their behalf. The letter was entrusted to one of Sir Richard's servants, who rode in haste towards Wales. But in Shropshire the messenger was stopped and examined, and the letter was taken from him. It was sent to the Bishop of Lichfield, the President of Wales, while Griffith – that was the messenger's name – was retained in gaol at Shrewsbury. The bishop forwarded the letter to Cromwell, and inquired what was to be done, so that Sir Richard never knew of his brother's message until it was too late.

While Anne's friends were prevented from acting in her favour, her enemies laboured to complete her ruin. They searched eagerly for evidence against her, and examined every one who seemed likely to know anything to her disadvantage. Sir William Fitzwilliam and Sir William Paulet, aided by Sir Edward Baynton, seem to have distinguished themselves in this way at Greenwich, where Anne's personal servants had remained. Cromwell went frequently to the Tower, and appears to have principally conducted such little examination of the prisoners as took place.

Anne herself was not examined any further. At first, orders had been issued that, except in the presence of Lady Kingston, she was to hold no communication with the four women deputed to serve her; but it was soon decided that this would neither be practicable nor expedient. So her attendants were allowed to talk with her, on condition that everything of any importance which she might say to them should be reported to the constable. In a state of hysterical excitement Anne was unable to weigh her words and to control her tongue. On the morning after her arrest she spoke of Noreys, and told Mrs Cosyns, one of her attendants, of the conversation she had had with him. She then talked of Weston, whose indiscretion she seemed greatly to fear. The whole conversation was immediately reported to Kingston, who in his turn sent an account of it to Cromwell. The consequence was that Sir Francis Weston went to swell the number of the prisoners at the Tower.

About the same time, on the afternoon of Thursday, 4 May, William Bryerton, one of the gentlemen of the king's chamber, was also arrested. Like Weston, Bryerton had grown up at court, where, before receiving the office he held at the time of his arrest, he had been a page and a groom of the privy chamber. He was of a good family; and his uncle, Sir William Bryerton, or Brereton, one of Henry's ablest captains, had done excellent service in Ireland. As young Bryerton had married a lady of small fortune – the widow of Sir John Savage – his position was not equal to that of Weston; but he was able to make a very good figure at court, and, like other light-hearted courtiers, he was much in the society of Anne and her friends. The immediate occasion of his arrest does not appear; it may have been some further indiscretion on the part of Anne, or some statement wrung from her former servants or others about court.

On the following day the list of prisoners was completed by the arrest of Thomas Wyatt, Anne's cousin, and Sir Richard Page. Wyatt, it will be remembered, had been suspected – if not more – of being Anne's lover before she yielded to the king. Sir Richard Page, a gentleman of the privy chamber, had been, like the other prisoners, on very friendly terms with Anne, to whom he had rendered sundry little services, which she had requited with gifts and otherwise. Besides the persons who were actually sent to prison, a good many others were bound under heavy fines to present themselves before Cromwell or before the royal council. They were thus kept in suspense and fear, and could not exert themselves in favour of the accused.

It now remained to prepare the indictments against such of the prisoners as were to be brought to trial. Besides Anne, five of them were singled out. Mark Smeton, who had already confessed that he had committed adultery with the queen, was one of them. It was necessary to bring him publicly to trial, for his confession was the only direct evidence against Anne which Cromwell was able to produce. By promises of pardon he might be induced both to plead guilty and to tell more than he had yet told, but condemned he must be. The other four were Lord Rochford, Noreys, Weston, and Bryerton. Cromwell fully understood that it would be most dangerous to allow these men to escape. Had it been Henry's intention, after the death of Anne, to effect a reconciliation with Rome, the three last named might have been allowed to escape; but if he wished to keep a middle course it was his interest to eliminate from the party of the reformation as many as possible of those who might drive it to extremes, and thereby force the government to lean to the other side. Besides, Rochford and Noreys, if released, would certainly try to avenge their own wrongs and the fate of Anne; and they would probably be aided by Weston and Bryerton. It was deemed advisable, therefore, that they should all die.

As to Wyatt, he does not seem to have been on very intimate terms with Anne for some years. He was arrested rather that he might give evidence than that he might be brought to trial; and a few days after his imprisonment Cromwell wrote to his father, Sir Henry Wyatt, that the young man would be spared. It was decided, too, that Sir Richard Page, who was connected with the Fitzwilliams and the Russells, should be allowed to escape.

The examination of the prisoners producing no further evidence, the bills of indictment were drawn up. The original documents are still preserved. There are two findings of the grand juries of Middlesex and Kent; and when read together they tell a very strange tale. Anne was accused of having repeatedly committed adultery with Henry Noreys, William Bryerton, Sir Francis Weston, and Smeton, and of having been repeatedly guilty of incest with her brother Lord Rochford. She was also accused of having conspired with these five men to bring about the death of the king, and of having said that she did not love him, and that after his death she would marry one of her lovers. It was set forth, moreover, that Anne and her confederates had by their misdeeds brought Henry into contempt and had slandered his issue, and that the sorrow caused by their treasonable behaviour had so injured his health as to put his life in danger.

If we consider this long and heavy charge, its improbability at once becomes apparent. It is unnecessary to dwell on the extreme corruption and coarseness which it presupposes in Anne and her lovers; for of the corruption and coarseness of Henry's court we have ample proof. But even if it be admitted that Anne was one of the most depraved women of an extremely base court, it is most unlikely that she behaved in the manner described in the two indictments. According to her accusers, she never acted on impulse, but invariably made cool arrangements with her lovers as to the place and time when and where she was to meet them, although, according to the very detailed accounts presented in the indictments, she ought to have thought herself unobserved and in no danger of surprise. She is charged, not with giving way to temptation gradually, but with plunging at once into a vicious life; and it is assumed that she was guilty of adultery within a month after the birth of Elizabeth, and of incest a month before she was delivered of her stillborn babe. There was no evidence whatever to support such accusations as these.

The second part of the indictment, that which relates to conspiring the king's death, is open to even greater doubt than the first. Towards the end of 1535, and in January 1536, Anne would have been inconceivably foolish had she wished Henry to die. In November Catherine was still in good health, and if Henry had suddenly died there would have been an immediate rising in favour of her and of her daughter. Anne would not have been able to offer even a semblance of resistance, Cromwell himself would have turned against her, Kingston would have shut the gates of the Tower in her face, and the gaolers at Kimbolton and Hatfield would have been the first to try to obtain forgiveness by raising the banner of Catherine and Mary.

At first sight it may seem that Anne was in less danger after Catherine's death. But Anne's enemies were exasperated by that event, and they drew together even more closely than they had done at any previous period. Besides, Anne had at that time the very best reasons for not risking anything. She was with child, and she knew that if she bore the king a son she would be safe. The pretended conspiracy to murder the king, and the alleged promise to marry one of her lovers, seem to have been nothing more than an amplification of Anne's conversation with Noreys at the end of April – the conversation of which she spoke the day after her committal to the Tower. Such amplifications were too common in the time of the Tudors.

But while I am strongly of opinion that the indictments were drawn up at random, and that there was no trustworthy evidence to sustain the specific charges, I am by no means convinced that Anne did not commit offences quite as grave as most of those of which she was accused. She may have been guilty of crimes which it did not suit the convenience of the government to divulge. At the subsequent trial some hints to this effect were thrown out, and although proof was not adduced they were likely enough to have been true.

8

Anne's Last Days

After leaving Greenwich on May Day, Henry went to York Place, his new palace at Westminster. Here he spent the night, and here on the following day Lord Rochford was arrested. It was at York Place, too, that Henry had the touching scene with the Duke of Richmond described in a former chapter.

The tears shed by the king over the danger which the Duke of Richmond had escaped did not flow long. They seem to have been the only tears the whole affair drew from his eyes, for on the following day he was in excellent spirits. Although accustomed to dissemble, he could not hide his joy that means had been found to rid him of Anne and to enable him to take a new wife. As he had allowed his exultation to appear at the death of Catherine, so he showed his delight at the coming fate of Anne. Never had the court been so lively as now, when the titular queen and some of the foremost courtiers lay in the Tower awaiting sentence of death. Feasts and banquets followed one another, and the inhabitants of the river-banks were often roused from their sleep by the music which enlivened Henry as he went home in his barge from some prolonged festivity.

Notwithstanding the coarseness of the age, notwithstanding the indifference of most people of the time to bloodshed, notwithstanding the hatred with which the Boleyns were regarded, Henry's raptures provoked general disgust. Even his courtiers disapproved of his behaviour, and although they vied with each other in providing amusement for him they spoke contemptuously of his merriment. Among others, the Bishop of Carlisle gave a supper to Henry and to some of the ladies at court. Here the king showed exuberant mirth. He spoke with the bishop of the arrest of Anne, and said he had long

foreseen that such would be her end. He had even written a tragedy
on the subject; and drawing a book out of his doublet he showed it
to the bishop. The latter went next day to see Chapuis and told him
of Henry's conduct, using expressions, it seems, not very flattering to
the king.

But Henry not only pretended that he had foreseen all that was
happening; it is evident that he took an active part in shaping the
course of future events. He was regularly informed of every step taken
against Anne and her associates, and he interfered a good deal with
the proceedings. Although, as on most other occasions, it was chiefly
about matters of detail he was asked to decide, his wishes probably
influenced the form in which the indictments were drawn up.

The indictments were to be laid before the two grand juries of
Middlesex and Kent, where the crimes were said to have been
committed. On 9 May precepts to this effect were addressed to the
sheriffs, Humphrey Monmouth and John Cotes for Middlesex, and
Sir Edward Wotton for Kent. They immediately returned a list of
jurors, of whom those for Middlesex were to attend at Westminster,
and those for Kent at Deptford. That these juries were packed there
is no reason to believe. It would have been quite superfluous to take
so much trouble, the proceedings before the grand jury being in such
cases considered a mere formality. Never had a bill presented by the
royal officials of the Tudors been ignored, and the confidence of the
government was so complete that the principal commissioners did
not even attend at the sitting. Only some of the judges presided; and
before them, on the 10th at Westminster, and on the 11th at Deptford,
true bills were found.

Even before the indictments had been found, the day for the trial
of the four commoners had been fixed. They were to be tried on
the morning of Friday the 12th, at Westminster Hall. On the 11th
Cromwell went to Hampton Court, to which Henry had retired, and
settled with the king the details of the coming trial, returning to town
in the evening. No one but the king and the secretary had anything
to do with the final arrangements. The Duke of Norfolk even, who
remained at court on the 11th, knew nothing of what was to happen
on the following day. Afraid to commit himself, he asked Sir William
Paulet how matters stood, but found him equally ignorant. The duke
declared he would not act without special orders from the king,

and sent a message to that effect to Cromwell. Shortly afterwards he received the news that he was expected to sit the next morning.

On Friday morning, then, the court over which Audley presided opened at Westminster Hall. With the exception of one of the judges, Sir Thomas Englefield, all the commissioners sat, Lord Wiltshire among them. The four prisoners were brought up by Sir William Kingston; and when the indictments had been read, they were asked whether they would plead guilty or not. Smeton, having already confessed the adultery, pleaded guilty as to this part of the charge, throwing himself on the mercy of the king. As to the rest of the charge he declared himself innocent. Noreys, Weston, and Bryerton pleaded not guilty to all the charges. A jury was immediately sworn to try the case. Here, I must say, the list looks rather suspicious. Of the twelve knights who composed the jury most were royal officials. Sir Thomas Wharton was comptroller in the north. Sir Richard Tempest, a near kinsman of Anne's aunt and enemy, Lady Boleyn, was steward of Wakefield and constable of Sandale. Sir William Musgrave was constable of Bewcastle and keeper of the park of Plumpton, and had a yearly pension of £20 out of the revenues of Sorby. Moreover, he had signed a bond for 2,000 marks to Cromwell and others the king's officers, payment of which might be demanded. Sir Thomas Palmer was one of the ushers of receipts of the exchequer. Sir Edward Willoughby was keeper of Hendley park. Sir William Sidney had been keeper of the great scales of London. Sir Walter Hungerford was the son-in-law of Lord Hussey, Anne's bitter enemy, and had just obtained from royal favour a writ of summons to the House of Lords. Sir Giles Alington was the son-in-law of Lady More, Sir Thomas More's widow. As to the four others, Sir William Askew, Robert Dormer, William Drewry, and John Hampden, I have found no proof of their holding any office or pension under the crown; but they had all been justices of the peace in their counties, some even sheriffs. They were, therefore, men trusted by the government.

Before such a jury the accused had but small chance. Even had the jurors felt no prejudice against Anne and her friends, they could not have approached the consideration of the case with perfect impartiality; for they knew that if they acquitted the three gentlemen they would draw on themselves the anger of the king and his ministers, and that in the event of Henry trying to take vengeance for their verdict they would not find any allies upon whom they could rely. Besides, in the time of the Tudors it was the accused person who had to prove his innocence rather than the king's officers who had to prove his guilt; and in this instance the prisoners were more than usually hampered in their defence. Until the indictments were read in court, they probably did not know the specific acts with which they were charged: and it was impossible for them, without preparation, to recall what had happened on the days when their offences were said to have been committed. Their condemnation was inevitable, and a verdict of guilty was returned on all counts. Sir Christopher Hales, the attorney-general, asked for judgment against Smeton on his own confession, against the other three on the verdict; and the court condemned them to suffer the usual torture and death as traitors.

It was now the turn of Anne and Rochford. But as it had become too late to call together a sufficient number of peers for the following day, their trial had to be postponed to Monday the 15th.

By this time Anne had somewhat recovered from the shock she had received on the day of her arrest. She was quieter, and we hear less of such hysterical attacks as were reported on the 3rd and 4th of May. It seems that she did not quite realise her position. She fancied that she was liked by the greater part of the English people, and hoped that the bishops preferred by her influence would interfere in her favour. She had not even heard of Cranmer's cowardice. As to the past she appears to have been undisturbed by scruples of conscience. She felt no remorse for the part she had taken against Catherine, Fisher, More, and the other martyrs; and at that time, and among persons of her class, any crimes of a different kind which she may have committed were scarcely considered to be morally wrong. What she remembered was her steady kindness to her friends and adherents; and she expressed a firm hope that if she died she would go straight to heaven.

It was only after she had been several days in the Tower that she heard that her brother lay a prisoner in a cell not far from her. She had probably expected as much, for when Kingston confirmed the news she showed no extraordinary emotion. At the same time she was told of the arrest of Weston, Bryerton, Wyatt, and Page. She manifested no fear of them, but chatted about them very freely with her gaolers. Of the two prisoners who escaped, Wyatt and Page, she seems to have said nothing that could expose them to danger.

Even in this time of dire distress Anne abated nothing of her overbearing temper. She had complained of the rudeness of the councillors at Greenwich; she now expressed her astonishment that they did not wait on her to hear her further defence. She complained, too, of the ladies whom the king had deputed to wait on her, and did not hide her dislike for them. Chapuis she greatly abused, ascribing chiefly to his influence the action that had been taken against her. Ever since he had been at court, on 18 April, she said, the king's manner towards her had altered.

In this way Anne spent her days in the Tower until the moment arrived for her trial. On 13 May the Duke of Norfolk, who had been named Lord High Steward of England for the occasion, issued a precept to summon twenty-six peers in or near London to appear on the 15th at the Tower, there to decide as a jury between Anne and Lord Rochford on the one hand and the king on the other. The peers thus summoned were the Duke of Suffolk, the Marquis of Exeter, the Earls of Arundel, Oxford, Northumberland, Westmoreland, Derby, Worcester, Rutland, Sussex, and Huntingdon, and the Lords Audeley, Lawarr, Mountague, Morley, Thomas Dacres of the South, Cobham, Maltravers, Powes, Mounteagle, Clinton, Sandys, Wyndsor, Wentworth, Burgh, and Mordaunt.

That this panel was quite fairly chosen I have no doubt. The whole lay peerage at that time consisted of sixty-two persons. Of these, four were women, and two under age. Four of the peers – the Earl of Kent, and Lords Dudley, Say, and Talboys – never sat, being too poor. The Earl of Cumberland and Lord Dacres of the North were employed on the marches towards Scotland, while Lord Lisle was deputy of Calais. The Duke of Norfolk acted as high steward. Of the remaining forty-six, excluding Lord Rochford and Lord Wiltshire, several had at their urgent request been excused from attending the parliament which was going to open, while twenty-six had been summoned and had appeared.

Among those who sat, there were, indeed, many enemies of Anne: the Duke of Suffolk, who had opposed her from the beginning, the Marquis of Exeter, Catherine's and Mary's staunch friend, the Earl of Northumberland, whose former passion for Anne had been changed into hatred, the Earl of Derby and the Lords Mountague and Sandys, who had joined the conspiracy against her. But, on the other hand, such bitter enemies of Anne as Lord Dacres of the North, Lord Hussey, Lord Bray, and Lord Darcy had not been summoned, as they would certainly have been if it had been thought necessary to have a packed jury. Probably the Duke of Norfolk omitted no peer whom he knew to be in or near London.

It was not thought fit that a woman who, according to the statutes, was still Queen of England, should be led as a prisoner through the city to Westminster. Anne and Rochford were, therefore, to be tried in the Tower, and the great hall was prepared for the court. A platform was erected, benches were made for the peers, a dais on which was a raised chair was spread for the high steward, and barriers were placed to keep off the crowd.

On Monday morning, 15 May, Norfolk and the peers took their seats. The Lord Chancellor Audley sat next to the duke, for although, as a commoner, he could not officially interfere, he might privately advise the high steward. Sir John Allen, the Lord Mayor, with a deputation of aldermen, wardens, and members of the principal crafts of London, attended by order of the king. The part of the hall not occupied by the court was crowded with people who wanted to see a queen of England tried for adultery and treason.

As soon as the members of the court had taken their places Anne, attended by Lady Kingston and Lady Boleyn, was brought in by Sir William Kingston and Sir Edmund Walsingham, the Lieutenant of the Tower. A chair had been provided for her, and she sat down to hear the indictments read. When the reading was over, and the usual question had been put to her, she pleaded not guilty. On behalf of the crown Sir Christopher Hales argued in favour of the indictments, and he was assisted by Cromwell, who, having formerly been a lawyer, appeared as counsel for the king. They did not keep strictly to the indictments, but heaped accusation upon accusation. Anne's conversation with Noreys, reported by Kingston, was adduced as evidence that she had agreed to marry Noreys after the king's death. From this it appeared that they desired his death; and this, again, was held to prove that they had conspired to bring it to pass. Besides arguing in this tortuous fashion, Hales and Cromwell brought forward new charges. They accused Anne of having given certain lockets to Noreys, from which they concluded that she had contrived to have Catherine poisoned, and had conspired to bring Mary to the same end. They furthermore asserted that she and her brother had spoken contemptuously of the king, of his literary productions, and of the way in which he dressed, and that she had shown that she was tired of him.

In the presence of immediate danger Anne regained her composure, and defended herself temperately and ably. She denied absolutely the crimes laid to her charge. That she had given money to Weston she admitted; but she had done the same to several other young courtiers – in their case, as in his, without any criminal intent. Although she was, of course, unable to produce rebutting evidence, she spoke so well, and so thoroughly upset the whole structure of the prosecution, that before an impartial tribunal she would scarcely have been convicted. But her efforts were of no avail. The question which presented itself to the minds of the lords was, not whether she was guilty of the charges contained in the indictments, but whether she was to die or not. This question they answered in the affirmative. After the pleadings they retired, and soon came back with a verdict of guilty.

The Duke of Norfolk thereupon gave sentence that Anne, Queen of England, was to be burnt or beheaded at the king's pleasure. She heard the sentence without shrinking, and having obtained leave to say a few words she declared that she did not fear to die. The thing which grieved her most, she asserted, was that the gentlemen included in the indictments, who were absolutely innocent, should suffer on her account, and all she asked was to be allowed a short time to prepare for death. Kingston and Walsingham then led their prisoner back to her apartment, and her place at the bar was taken by her brother. Before his trial began, however, the Earl of Northumberland was obliged, by illness, to leave the Tower. He was dying of a nervous disorder, and it may be that although he had hated Anne of late most cordially, he felt some compunction for condemning her to death. The court went on with its work without him.

Rochford was accused of having on one occasion remained a long time in Anne's room; and against charges of this kind, which were neither authenticated nor proof of guilt, he defended himself energetically. To the charge that he had used expressions showing that he doubted whether Elizabeth was Henry's child, he made no reply. Rash, overbearing, and mocking as he and Anne were, he may have uttered some such jest; and he was now to pay for it with his life. In the course of his trial it was asserted that Anne had told Lady Rochford that Henry was no longer able to beget children. This statement, which Cromwell did not wish to be made public, was written on a piece of paper, and handed to the accused, who was forbidden to read it aloud. But Rochford, having become fully aware that there was no hope of pardon, disregarded the prohibition, and loudly proclaimed the contents of the sheet.

After the matter had been argued at great length, Rochford defending himself cleverly and stoutly, the peers were once more called upon to pronounce their verdict, and in answer to Norfolk they found the accused guilty on all counts. Judgement was given, and then Lord Rochford was allowed to speak a few words. He said in general terms that he was worthy to die, but he craved from the king's mercy that his debts might be paid out of his fortune, which was by the judgment forfeited to the crown. After this he was taken back to his cell, and the court rose.

The condemnation of Anne had been generally expected, but it had been believed that her brother would be acquitted. At the trial he defended himself so vigorously and so eloquently, that among the common people who were present wagers were laid at ten to one that he would get off. The fact was that during the last few days there had been a strong revulsion of popular feeling. At first the downfall of the chiefs of the Boleyn faction had been hailed with joy by all whom their pride and insolence had galled, by every one who expected some share in the plunder that was likely to be divided after such a catastrophe, and by those who hoped that there would now be a complete political and religious reaction. It had been assumed that there was some real foundation for the charges brought against the prisoners; beyond a very limited circle no one knew the exact nature of the crimes of which they were accused, or the kind of evidence that was to be adduced in proof.

The trial of the commoners at Westminster disclosed the true state of affairs. For the first time the English people heard of the charge of incest, which, even in so corrupt a society as that of Henry's court, was considered almost incredible. The public, too, were gravely informed that Henry had taken the infidelity of the queen so much to heart, had felt such overwhelming sorrow, that his health had been injured. This they were told at the very time when they heard the sounds of rejoicing coming from the royal barge, when Henry was known to be in unusually high spirits. Moreover, the king's dallying with Jane Seymour, which now began to be talked about, raised a suspicion that Anne was to die in order to make way for an equally depraved rival. When all these considerations were added to that feeling of good nature which impels Englishmen to spare a vanquished foe and to favour the weaker party, the unpopularity of Anne soon decreased. Many of those who had been most furious against her became anxious that no harm should be done either to her or to Rochford.

But there was no hope for any of the prisoners. An attempt was made to save Sir Francis Weston, whose family was powerful and rich, and had generally sided against the Boleyns. The French ambassadors are said to have interfered in his favour, but their request – if made – was not granted. On the day after the trial of Anne and Rochford, the five men condemned to suffer death were told to prepare for execution on the following morning. This they did as well as they could. They confessed, made out lists of their debts, and wrote farewell letters to their families, whom, it appears, they were not permitted to see. One of these farewell letters, that of Sir Francis Weston, has been preserved at the Record Office. It is written at the end of the list of his debts, amounting in all to about £900. It runs:

> Father and mother and wife, I shall humbly desire you for the salvation of my soul to discharge me of this bill, and for to forgive me of all my offences that I have done to you, and in especial my wife, which I desire for the love of God to forgive me and to pray for me, for I believe prayer will do me good. God's blessing have my children and mine. By me a great offender to God.

By royal order the scaffold was prepared, not at Tyburn, but on Tower Hill; and instead of being hanged, disembowelled, and quartered, the prisoners were simply to be beheaded. They were allowed to address the people, who had come in great numbers to witness their execution. Except in the case of Lord Rochford, of whose words conflicting versions remain, their speeches have not been preserved. So much, however, seems certain, that the prisoners did not assert their innocence, but that on the other hand not one of them confessed that he had been guilty of those offences for which he had been condemned. The former fact has been held to prove that they virtually admitted their guilt; but this is not a legitimate inference. On such occasions condemned persons were permitted to speak only if they promised not to say anything against the king or in opposition to the sentence they had received; and up to the last moment the government had very effectual means of enforcing the covenant. For it might interrupt the execution, and order an offender to be hanged, drawn and quartered; or his family might be made to smart for the violation of his pledge. Hence scarcely any of Henry's victims dared to maintain their innocence. When Lady Salisbury did so in 1541 she was considered by the government to have been guilty of an extraordinary piece of impertinence; and her family might have fared ill had any of them remained in the king's power.

So Lord Rochford, Weston, Noreys, Bryerton, and Smeton were executed on Wednesday 17 May. Their bodies were exposed to no further ignominy, but thrown into simple shells and buried in the Tower.

Meanwhile, attempts had been made to secure the aid of Anne for the accomplishment of a scheme in which the king was profoundly interested. Having no legitimate heir male, and being in doubt whether Jane Seymour would ever contrive to bear him a son, Henry had begun to think of his bastard son, Henry Fitzroy, Duke of Richmond. It occurred to him that if he had no legitimate male offspring it might be possible to obtain the sanction of parliament for the recognition of the duke as heir to the crown. But as yet little Elizabeth stood in the way; she had been solemnly proclaimed heir presumptive, and her title could not be easily disregarded. It was desirable, therefore, that Anne's daughter should be declared illegitimate.

This object might have been attained if Henry had been willing to adduce proof that Elizabeth was not his child. The words attributed to Rochford, whether really spoken or not, and the general rumour that Elizabeth was the daughter of Noreys, would have been held sufficient evidence by a subservient primate and a willing parliament.

But Henry would not hear of this; he insisted that Elizabeth should be recognised as his daughter, yet be proclaimed a bastard. This was, of course, impossible, unless it were decreed that his marriage with Anne Boleyn had been invalid from the beginning. In support of such a decree Henry might have used the argument which in the opinion of nearly every foreigner and of most Englishmen was the best, namely, that he was legally and validly married to Catherine when he took Anne for his wife. But had this reason been advanced, he would have acknowledged that he had been guilty of adultery or bigamy, and that he had been in the wrong, and had shown bad faith throughout the whole of the proceedings connected with the divorce case. Moreover, by a divorce from Anne based on this ground Mary would have been declared legitimate.

This argument being considered inadmissible, the statements of the Countess of Northumberland with regard to a previous marriage, or a binding precontract, on the part of Anne, were remembered, and Cromwell was directed to follow up the matter. On Saturday 13 May, the day after the condemnation of the commoners, Sir Raynold Carnaby, a friend of Northumberland, was sent to him to obtain if possible a retractation of what he had formerly said, and an admission that there had been a precontract between him and Anne. But the earl either had spoken the truth and honestly adhered to it, or he was aware that he would put himself in serious danger by making such a confession as was desired. If a precontract existed, his denial of it before the king's marriage with Anne might well have been construed as an act of treason. So he stoutly upheld his former deposition before Warham, Lee, and the council, that there was no precontract between him and the queen.

There remained but one other conceivable reason for a divorce – a forbidden degree of affinity. Now Mary Boleyn, Anne's sister, had been Henry's mistress; and as illegitimate relations, according to the canon law, formed as strong an obstacle as legitimate relations, there was a forbidden degree. Scandalous as the proceeding might be, the marriage was to be annulled on this ground.

The person who was required by the new rules to pronounce sentence was Anne's friend, Thomas Cranmer. However loth he might be to take an active part against his former patron, however annoyed at having to declare invalid that which he had solemnly declared to be valid, he had no choice. He knew that the king might undo him at any moment; he had been sufficiently frightened by Cromwell's peremptory messages; he was ready for anything that might be asked of him. On the morning of the day following the trial of Anne he went to the Tower, and was admitted to her presence. What he told her and what she said to him is not known; but when he left her, she was convinced that she would be pardoned and allowed to leave the country. She told the ladies who were guarding her, that she would be sent to Antwerp. It is, therefore, probable that the primate gave her hopes that her life might be spared if she would consent to a divorce.

On the 17th, at nine o'clock in the morning, the primate opened his court at Lambeth. The Lord Chancellor, the Duke of Suffolk, the Earls of Oxford and of Sussex, Sir Thomas Cromwell, and others of the king's council were present. Doctor Richard Sampson appeared for the king, Doctors Nicholas Wotton and John Barbour for Anne. Whether the two latter had really received any powers from her does not appear. They may have been named by Henry in accordance with the precedent set in 1527 on the occasion of the collusive suit against Catherine; but, on the other hand, it is not improbable that one of Cranmer's objects in going to see Anne at the Tower was to induce her to appoint Wotton and Barbour as her proctors.

In any case the two men who appeared for Anne did nothing to defend her cause. Had they had the interest of their client at heart, they might have raised such difficulties that, if Henry had obstinately insisted on securing a divorce, he would have been compelled to come to terms with Anne in order to obtain her consent, and thus her life might have been spared. But Wotton and Barbour were royal officials, anxious to please the king; so Cranmer was allowed to give sentence. He solemnly declared the marriage between Henry and Anne to have been null and invalid from the beginning.

Anne might now be allowed to die. Her hopes of life had not lasted long, for Kingston had soon undeceived her. After the sitting at Lambeth her execution was fixed for the morning of the 18th, and she was told of it. She slept little that night; her almoner was in attendance, and from two o'clock onwards she remained in prayer with him. In the morning she sent for Kingston, and asked him to be present when she was to receive the sacrament and to assert her innocence of the crimes laid to her charge. Shortly afterwards the communion was celebrated, and both before and after receiving the host she declared on the salvation of her soul that she had never been unfaithful to the king. After this she patiently waited; but as time passed on she became restless, and asked her attendants when she was to die. They answered that she would not be executed before noon. In reality, the execution was not to take place until the following day.

The explanation of this change of plan is not perfectly clear. It seems that Anne, faithful to her French education, considered it more honourable to die by the stroke of a sword than to have her head hacked off with an axe. The hangman of Calais, the only subject of Henry who knew how to behead with a sword, had, therefore, been sent for; and he may not have arrived at the expected time. It is more probable, however, that the delay was due to a different cause.

The government now regretted that so many people had been allowed to hear the incredible accusations against Anne and her brother, and their able and eloquent defence. Many strangers had been present at the trials; and it was feared that after their return to their homes they would give a very unfavourable account of the king's proceedings. On Thursday morning, therefore, Cromwell wrote to Kingston that all foreigners were to be expelled from the Tower. In reporting that this order had been obeyed, Kingston expressed the opinion that if the exact time was not made public there would probably be few spectators; and it is not unlikely that the government decided to postpone the execution in the hope that this suggestion would prove to be right.

When Anne's attendants told her that she would not die before noon, she sent for Kingston and complained to him of the delay. She had hoped, she said, to be past her pain. The constable tried to console her; it was no pain, he said, it was so quickly done. Anne spoke of the executioner's skill and of the smallness of her neck; and then, the long waiting having unstrung her nerves, she had another attack of hysterical laughter, by which the constable was sorely puzzled. 'I have seen many men and also women executed,' he wrote, 'and that they have been in great sorrow; and to my knowledge this lady has much joy and pleasure in death.' The rest of the day Anne spent partly in praying, partly in chatting with her attendants on her past life and on her future fame. Those ingenious persons, she said, who had forged so infamous a name for the late queen would have no trouble in finding one for her. They would call her Queen Lackhead. And therewith came another burst of hysterical laughter. There was but one thing which preyed on her mind, her behaviour to the Princess Mary. She repeatedly spoke of it, saying that she had been brought to this end by divine judgment for being the cause of Mary's ill-treatment and for having tried to bring about her death. Of the common story that Anne, kneeling, asked Lady Kingston to beg Mary to pardon her, I have found no trace; and it may be dismissed as an embellishment of later writers.

In this way the time went on. During the night Anne seems to have taken scarcely any rest, her nerves being too excited for sleep. She continued to talk to her ladies, and conversed and prayed with her almoner. As the morning of Friday 19 May approached, Kingston informed her that she would shortly be executed, and he handed her a purse with £20 which she was to distribute, according to custom, as alms before her death. A little before nine he returned, and announced that the moment had come.

During the night a platform had been erected in the courtyard of the Tower. It rose but a few feet above the ground, for it had been deemed inexpedient to raise a high scaffold which might be seen from afar. In the courtyard the Lord Chancellor, the Dukes of Suffolk and of Richmond, Sir Thomas Cromwell, and others of the council were assembled to witness Anne's death. The Lord Mayor, with some aldermen and representatives of the crafts of the city, attended by order; and as their coming had attracted attention, they had been followed by a considerable number of people. But strict watch had been kept at the gates, and although Englishmen had been freely admitted, all foreigners had been excluded.

Anne now appeared, led by Kingston and followed by the four ladies. She wore a dressing-gown of grey damask, which she had chosen because it was low round the neck and would not interfere with the executioner's work. For the same reason she had tied up her hair in a net, over which she wore the customary head-dress. In this guise she was handed over by Kingston to the sheriffs, who led her up to the platform.

Permission was granted to her to address the crowd, and she did so in few words and very simply. She had not come to preach, she said, but to die. She asked those who were present to pray for the king, who was a right gentle prince and had treated her as well as possible. She said that she accused nobody on account of her death, for she had been sentenced according to the law of the country. So she was ready to die, and asked the forgiveness of all whom she might have wronged. Having said these words, she herself took off her head-dress, which she handed to one of the ladies. Then she once more asked the bystanders to pray to God for her.

During the whole time that she had been on the scaffold, she had been nervously looking round towards the place where the executioner stood leaning on his heavy sword, Now she knelt down, and one of her attendants bound a handkerchief round her eyes. After this the ladies also knelt down, silently praying, while she repeated the words: 'Oh God, have pity on my soul.' The executioner stepped quickly forward and took his aim; the heavy two handled blade flew hissing through the air, and Anne's head rolled in the dust.

Head and trunk were taken up by the ladies, wrapped in a sheet, laid in a plain coffin, and carried to the Tower chapel. Here they were buried with little ceremony. No inscription, except a few letters, was put upon Anne's grave, and the exact spot was soon forgotten. It was discovered only a few years ago.

Such was the end of a strange and eventful career. For a moment it seemed as if Anne would leave no trace in history; but the schism of which she had been the first cause, and to which in one form or another the ruling powers were already deeply committed, could not be undone. Her influence survived, too, in the little girl at Hunsdon, who grew up to be very like her, although Elizabeth never showed a spark of tenderness for the memory of her mother and would have been ashamed to own that she resembled her. From Anne the English people received one of the greatest of their rulers, and for this gift they may well forgive such misdeeds as were not atoned for by long and cruel anxiety and a terrible death. Anne was not good; she was incredibly vain, ambitious, unscrupulous, coarse, fierce, and relentless. But much of this was due to the degrading influences by which she was surrounded in youth and after her return to England from France. Her virtues, such as they were, were her own. So we may pass no harsher judgment on her than was passed by Cromwell when, speaking confidentially to Chapuis of the woman whose destruction he had wrought, he could not refrain from extolling her courage and intelligence. Among her good qualities he might also have included her warm and constant attachment to her friends.

9

Conclusion

For more than a week after Anne's arrest, the English government remained silent as to the causes which had led to it and to the imprisonment of so many other persons of note. This reticence gave rise to such very extraordinary rumours both at home and abroad, that Cromwell at last thought it wiser to inform the English agents at foreign courts how the matter was to be spoken of. On 14 May he wrote to Gardiner and Wallop:

The queen's abomination, both in inconvenient living and other offences towards the king's highness was so rank and common that her ladies of her privy chamber and her chamberers could not contain it within their breasts, but, detesting the same, had so often consultations and conferences of it, that at last it came so plainly to the ears of some of his grace's council that with their duty to his majesty they could not conceal it from him, but with great fear, as the case enforced, declared what they heard unto his highness. Whereupon in most secret sort certain persons of the privy chamber and others of her side were examined, in which examination the matter appeared so evident, that besides that crime with the accidents, there broke out a certain conspiracy of the king's death, which extended so far that all we, that had the examination of it, quaked at the danger his grace was in, and on our knees gave Him laud and praise that he had preserved him so long from it and now manifested the most wretched and detested determination of the same. Then were certain men committed to the Tower for this cause: that is Marke and Norres, and her brother; then was she apprehended and conveyed to the same place; after her was sent thither, for the crimes specified, Sir Francis Weston and William Brereton. And Norres, Weston, Brereton and Mark be already condemned to death upon arraignment in Westminster Hall on Friday last. She and her brother shall be arraigned tomorrow and will undoubtedly go the same way. I write no particularities, the things be so abominable, and therefore I doubt not but this shall be sufficient instruction to declare the truth if you have occasion so to do.

Similar accounts were published in England, but the people declined to believe the official version, and continued secretly to blame the government for the way in which the trials had been conducted. After a time their interest in Anne's fate died out, but a few of her adherents always held her memory dear, and we find among the records of the following years a note or two of proceedings against persons who maintained that Henry had put her to death unjustly. In France poems were written in her honour, and in Germany the Protestants expressed strong disapproval of the king's act. About 1544, Jean de Luxembourg, Abbot of Ivry, wrote an *Oraison de Madame Marie de Cleves*, in which it is said that Henry was suspected of having already ill-treated, that is to say murdered, three wives. And Constantine, in his memorial, reports a saying of the councillors of the Duchess of Milan to the effect that 'her great aunte was poisoned, that the second was innocently put to death, and the third lost for lack of keeping in her childbed'. By and by, however, those who had known Anne passed away, the real person was forgotten, and fantastic portraits of her were drawn both by admirers and by enemies. And so her history was distorted by party spirit until it became a mere myth.

The fortnight before Anne's execution Henry had spent in the most pleasant manner. After a short stay at York Place he went to Hampton Court, and Jane Seymour was sent to a house of Sir Nicholas Carew, about seven miles from London. Here the king frequently visited her, but he soon found that the distance was too great. On 14 May she removed to a house on the Thames, only a mile from the court; and in this residence she was served with quasi-regal pomp, having numerous servants and living in splendid style. On the 15th she received a message from the king that at three in the afternoon she would hear of Anne's condemnation; and shortly after dinner, Sir Francis Bryan, Anne's cousin, arrived with the welcome intelligence.

When, on the Friday following, the death of Anne was announced to Henry, he immediately took his barge and went to spend the day with Jane Seymour at the place where she lived. Next morning, at six o'clock, she secretly joined him at Hampton Court, and there, in the presence of a few courtiers, they were married. A few days later the marriage was acknowledged, and Jane appeared as queen.

The hopes entertained by the conservative and papal party after the arrest of Anne were doomed to disappointment. The first news of her imprisonment reached Rome by way of Flanders, about the middle of May. Paul III at once sent for Gregorio da Casale, and told him what had happened, saying that God had enlightened the conscience of Henry. The pope showed himself most anxious for a reconciliation, and eagerly pointed out to Casale that by forming an alliance with the Holy See, Henry would gain so much authority that he might lay down the law both to Charles V and to Francis. He, the pope, had always been at heart Henry's friend, and whatever he had done against him he had been forced to do. The slightest advance Henry might make would be gladly responded to.

Casale asked the pope whether he might write all this to the King of England; but Paul III replied that if after the insults and injuries he had received he took the first step in the matter, people would cry shame on him. Casale was to keep everything that had been said strictly secret; he was only to assure his employers of the pope's goodwill, and to urge them not to miss so fortunate an opportunity of making peace with the papacy. If Paul III saw any favourable sign, he would send Messer Latino Juvenale, Casale's uncle, or some other agent, to England, who would go nominally for the purpose of transacting some private business of his own.

Notwithstanding the pope's request that the conversation should be kept secret, Casale gave Henry a full account of it; and he expressed a hope that the intended mission of Latino Juvenale would not be prevented, as it could do no harm and might do good. Casale seems to have encouraged the friendly disposition of the pope; for little more than a week after the date of his letter an agent was despatched to England.

The person chosen for this errand was Marco Antonio Campeggio. He received his instructions from his brother, Cardinal Campeggio, who had acted as papal legate in the time of Wolsey. He was to ask that the cardinal should be reinstated in the revenues of his former see of Salisbury; but this was to be only the ostensible occasion of his visit. If a favourable chance offered itself, he was to urge on the royal ministers that for the honour of God and the quiet of the realm the king ought to seek for a reconciliation with the Holy See, which would deal with him graciously. Henry was to be advised to give proof of a friendly temper by repressing the preaching of new heresies, and to obtain peace of conscience by begging for absolution for his offences, as his predecessors had often done, earning thereby praise and glory. Those whom Marco Antonio would find favourable were the Dukes of Norfolk and Suffolk, the Bishops of Durham and Winchester, and Campeggio's agent.

As these instructions are now in the British Museum among the Cotton Manuscripts, they must have been formerly at the State-paper Office; and from this I conclude that Marco Antonio really came to England and negotiated with the English ministers. This opinion is confirmed by the fact that at the Record Office there is a letter from Cardinal Campeggio to the Duke of Suffolk, accrediting Marco Antonio.

The pope not only tried direct offers, he had recourse to indirect means. He spoke with Denonville and with Nicolas Raince, strongly advocating the marriage of Henry and the Princess Madeleine of France. Raince wrote to Cardinal du Bellay that the pope had referred to this proposal again and again, and that his holiness could think of no more effectual way of obtaining a hold over the King of England.

But on the day after the departure of Marco Antonio Campeggio, Denonville received letters from England in which it was said that Henry again intended to marry one of his own subjects. Nicolas Raince mentioned this to the pope, who was greatly disappointed. Paul III continued, however, to believe that the French match might be brought about. A few days later he spoke of a marriage between the dauphin and the Princess Mary; and Denonville and Raince wrote about it to the French court.

It was only in July, presumably after he had heard from Marco Antonio, that the pope understood that Henry was not inclined to give up the spiritual supremacy he had arrogated to himself, and that he did not propose either to ask for absolution or to submit in any way to Rome. Paul III then spoke angrily of Henry and even more angrily of Cromwell, and abandoned all hope of regaining the allegiance of England by peaceful means.

Francis I also heard with annoyance of Henry's marriage with Jane, for – apart from his apparent desire to have the King of England for his son-in-law – he probably foresaw that Henry would soon be perfectly reconciled with the emperor, and that he himself would thereby lose a valuable ally and client. This anticipation was realised. After some time Charles was on very good terms with Henry, although he never gave up his defence of the memory of his aunt. For many years he and Queen Mary of Hungary irritated Henry by addressing him as 'wellbeloved uncle', and it was with great difficulty that Chapuis at last persuaded them to give up the use of the obnoxious name.

Mary gained little by the death of Anne. Contrary to the general expectation, Henry refused to admit her legitimacy or to restore her to her former rank. The Duke of Richmond soon died, but as long as he lived Henry appears to have wished to make him his successor, and Mary could escape the danger of imprisonment and death only by laying aside her pretensions to be the Princess of England. During the whole of Henry's reign she continued to play with the idea of flight and of rebellion, but even when the means were at her disposal she shrank from carrying out her purpose.

To Henry's courtiers the death of Rochford and his friends brought a golden harvest. Rochford and Noreys, being royal favourites, had enjoyed numerous pensions and a good many lucrative sinecures. As soon, therefore, as it was known that they had been arrested, an active correspondence took place regarding the sharing of the spoil.

To Gardiner and Wallop Cromwell wrote: 'Your lordship shall get in CC £ of the III that were out among these men… the 3rd C is bestowed of the vicar of hell.' At the end of the letter he added: 'And you master Wallop shall not at this time be forgotten, but the certainty of that ye shall have I cannot tell.'Gardiner was by no means satisfied with this arrangement. In 1529, Wolsey had been forced to grant to Rochford and Noreys pensions for life of £200 and £100, out of the revenues of Winchester. These pensions Gardiner had been obliged to pay, but now that the pensioners were to die the bishop thought that all the payments should cease. He protested in vain, however; he was even sharply reprimanded for complaining, and the 'vicar of hell', as Sir Francis Bryan was called, got his pension. What was the share of Sir John Wallop, I have not been able to make out.

The Duke of Richmond was not quick enough. He wrote on the 8th to the Bishop of Lincoln to secure the office of Steward of Banbury held by Noreys. But, three days before, the bishop had already offered it, with the stewardship of the university of Cambridge, to Cromwell. Robert Barnes applied for the mastership of Bedlam, worth, as he said, but £40. The other offices of the five men executed on 17 May were distributed in a similar manner.

In the summer of 1536, seeing that the change of queens had made no great change in politics, the conspirators rose against the king. But they had waited too long. The emperor gave them no help, for he was fully occupied in Provence, and at that very time he was treating with Henry about an alliance against France. Besides, many of the great lords had become reconciled to the new order of things, which, after all, they found rather profitable. Most of them had received considerable grants out of the lands of the dissolved abbeys; and they hoped that their chances of sharing in the spoil were not even yet exhausted. Moreover, the insurgents were embarrassed by the indecision and stupidity of Mary. She had scruples about encouraging open rebellion against her father; and the majority of her personal friends, knowing her mind, held back from the insurrection. The pilgrimage of grace, therefore, was suppressed with comparative ease, and Lord Darcy, Lord Hussey, and many other adherents of Mary were brought to the block.

Chapuis remained for several years as ambassador at the English court, on excellent terms with Henry and with his principal advisers. In the beginning of 1539, the relations between Charles and Henry having become less friendly, he was recalled, and the Dean of Cambray took his place. When the coldness passed away, and the emperor desired once more to be on good terms with Henry, Chapuis returned to England; and he remained there until the king crossed to Calais to take the command of his army before Boulogne. Chapuis was present at the siege, and after the campaign he went back with Francis van der Dilft, who had been chosen to succeed him as ambassador. Having spent more than four months in schooling van der Dilft for his new post, he had a farewell audience of the king, on 4 May 1545; and Henry did not conceal his regret, for he had come to like the man by whom he had been so ably and so stoutly resisted. At this time Chapuis was ill and crippled by gout; but he was still vigorous enough to be employed in treating with the English commissioners in the Low Countries. The last mention of him I have found is in 1546; the date of his death I do not know.

All of Henry's German favourites, Juergen Wullenwever, Dr Adam von Pack, and Marcus and Gerhard Meyer came to a violent end. Having been kept for many months a close prisoner, first at Rotenburg and afterwards at Steinbrueck, Wullenwever was brought to Wolfenbuettel, where, on 24 September 1537, he was sentenced to death and immediately executed. Doctor Pack left Hamburg in March 1536, to return to England; but while passing through the Low Countries he was detained and thrown into prison. At first Cromwell protested so strongly against his arrest that Chapuis wrote to Flanders; and on 16 April he wished to explain why the doctor had been seized. But having by this time heard of the proposals of Charles V, Cromwell did not want to quarrel about minor points; so he interrupted the ambassador with the remark that these were small matters of no importance. The authorities of the Low Countries, finding that Pack was to be left to his fate, tried to extort information from him by putting him to the rack, and soon afterwards he died in prison.

Marcus Meyer held out at Warberg for some time after Henry abandoned him; but in May he was obliged to surrender. In direct violation of the terms on which he capitulated, he was tried by a tribunal of his worst enemies, condemned, and executed. A few weeks later his brother Gerhard shared his fate.

And now I close these pages. My object has been to show that very little is known of the events of those times, and that the history of Henry's first divorce and of the rise and fall of Anne Boleyn has still to be written. If I have contributed to dispel a few errors, or have in any way helped towards the desired end, I shall be satisfied. The task I set myself will have been fulfilled.

Arrest of Anne & Her Accomplices

With regard to the real cause of Anne's fall, the correspondence of Chapuis has cleared up all doubt. But there still remains the question: What reasons did the government put forward to justify the arrest of the woman whom they called the queen, and of her friends?

There is an old story that Lady Wingfield, on her deathbed, revealed the crimes of Anne, and that it was upon this information that the government acted. It is not said by whom the deposition of Lady Wingfield was taken, nor how it was transmitted to the king. The story presents a good many difficulties, and it is made all the more improbable by the fact that in contemporary accounts no mention is made of any such deposition.

Chapuis gives no information on the subject, except that he expresses strong disapproval of the manner in which the trial was conducted, and censures the fact that depositions were not produced against the prisoners. The writer of the French life of Anne Boleyn gives a very strange and highly-coloured account. One of the members of the privy council, he says, had to reprove his sister for being too exuberant. The lady, seeing her fault discovered, tried to palliate her guilt by saying that the queen did much worse, and that Mark Smeton might tell the whole story of her scandalous life. The privy councillor was much frightened by this speech, for, on the one hand, if he kept the facts secret he might afterwards be blamed and punished; on the other hand, if he revealed them, he might be accused of slandering the king's issue. He took the advice of two of his friends, most intimate servants of the king; and in the end all three went to Henry and told him what they had heard. The king ordered them to be silent, and caused Anne to be watched and finally arrested.

According to a French manuscript printed by Mr Pocock, the gentleman in question was Anthony Brown, wrongly said to be the king's physician, and his sister had formerly been a mistress of the king. The writer of this paper certainly had access to some documents or other good sources; nevertheless I am not satisfied of the truth of the French accounts. They may be merely a reproduction of one of the many stories that were current at the time both at home and abroad.

The author of the Spanish Cronica del Rey Enrico otavo reports the story which seems to have been accepted by the Spanish merchants who resided in London towards the close of Henry's reign. He gives a very detailed account of the proceedings. Smeton, he says, was the last of Anne's lovers, and an old woman called Marguerita, servant to Anne, acted as their confidente. Having before that time been rather poor, Mark received considerable gifts from Anne, which he spent on dress, horses, and other showy objects. He became very overbearing, and treated the other courtiers with insolence. Finally he had a violent quarrel with Thomas Percy, who complained of him. Anne, on hearing of this, sent for Percy and ordered him to make up his quarrel with Mark. Percy was forced to obey, but, bearing the other a grudge, he went to Cromwell, told him of what Anne had done for Mark, and pointed out that the musician could not have by perfectly fair means all the money he was in the habit of spending. Cromwell thereupon asked Percy secretly to watch his enemy, which Percy did; and the result was, that, on 29 April, early in the morning, he saw Mark coming out of Anne's apartment. This he reported to the secretary; and on May Day, in the morning, Cromwell sent for Mark, and subjected him to torture by causing a knotted cord to be violently tightened round his head. Mark, unable to bear the pain, confessed, and said that Noreys and Bryerton had been his rivals. Cromwell wrote down the confession, and sent it to Henry at Greenwich, who received it in the afternoon, and immediately took his barge and left for Westminster. Noreys and Bryerton were secretly arrested, and Wyatt was also sent to the Tower, but treated with great kindness, Cromwell being his friend. The next day Anne and the duke her brother were arrested; and Anne was examined by Cranmer, the chancellor, Norfolk, and Cromwell. By and by she and her brother were sent to the Tower. Then the old woman Marguerita was arrested and put to the rack, when she incriminated Noreys and Bryerton, but swore that Wyatt was innocent. Rochford, Noreys, Bryerton and Mark were all condemned, and executed together; the old woman was burnt at night within the Tower; and Anne after her conviction was beheaded with a sword by the executioner of Saint Omer.

In many particulars this account is of course false. The writer knows nothing of Weston, he calls Rochford a duke, he makes Cranmer the president of the committee before which Anne appeared, and he falls into other and even greater mistakes. He has heard of Mistress Margaret, but he believes her to be an old woman, and evidently confounds her with the Lady Wingfield of Spelman.

The parts of the story, however, which relate to the insolence of Smeton, to his quarrel with Thomas Percy – there was a Sir Thomas Percy at court, brother of the Earl of Northumberland – and to his arrest and extorted confession, may well be true. They perfectly agree with the account of Constantine and with the official account of Cromwell.

Mr Froude, in the Appendix to the second volume of his History of England, gives one more version of the proximate cause of Anne's arrest. 'Lord Howard,' he says, 'wrote at the same time to Granvelle saying that he understood the "concubine" had been surprised in bed with the king's organist.' In proof of this statement about Lord Howard, Mr Froude quotes the following passage: 'Le visconte Howard a escript a Sr de Granvelle que au mesme instant il avoit entendu de bon lieu que la concubine dudict Roy avoit este surprise couchée avec l'organiste dudict Roy.' Unhappily Mr Froude does not say who was the writer of this extraordinary passage, to whom it was addressed, and where it may be found. Moreover, absolutely nothing is known of the existence of a 'Viscount Howard' in the time Henry VIII. There was a Lord Howard, but as he was also the Duke of Norfolk, he was always called by the latter title.

The official account of the causes of Anne's arrest does not go into details. In the letter written on 14 May to Gardiner and Wallop, Cromwell does not name the persons who first denounced Anne. He says her servants could not hide 'the queen's abomination' any longer;

and this perfectly agrees with the Spanish account. Cromwell further says that her servants and others were most secretly examined. This, again, agrees with the account of the chronicler and of Constantine. The plot to murder Henry is, of course, an embellishment of Cromwell's. On the whole, the statements of Cromwell, Constantine, and the Spanish chronicler support each other so well that the balance of evidence seems to be decidedly in favour of the account I have given in the text.

The order in which the arrests were made is now pretty certain. The first arrested was certainly Mark Smeton. This appears from Constantine's account, corroborated by Cromwell's, Chapuis's and Bulkeley's letters, as well as from the Histoire de Anne de Boullant, from the French account printed by Mr Pocock, and from the Spanish chronicle. Noreys was certainly arrested on the evening of May Day; Rochford on 2 May about noon. Anne was called before the council in the morning, and taken to the Tower about two o'clock in the afternoon. Weston and Bryerton were both arrested on Thursday 4 May. In the account of Constantine, printed in the Archæologia, Bryerton is said to have been arrested on Thursday afore May Day. But from the context it is clear that Bryerton was arrested after the other men were in the Tower, so that afore is either a clerical error or a misprint for after. Any doubt on this head is dispelled by Cromwell's letter to Gardiner and Wallop. As to Page and Wyatt, they seem to have been arrested about the same time as Bryerton and Weston, or at latest on the day following; for it appears from the letter of Kingston to Cromwell that Anne was told of the arrest of the two former on the same occasion on which she was told of that of Rochford and the two latter gentlemen.

According to the writer of the Spanish chronicle, Wyatt was told on the day before the execution of Rochford – that is, on the day after the conviction of Anne – that he would not be proceeded against. Thereupon, the chronicle proceeds, Wyatt wrote a letter to the king; and in this letter he took credit for having warned Henry not to marry Anne Boleyn, because she was a bad woman. For his boldness he had been banished from court for two years. Now he wished to state that his reason for speaking as he had done was that Anne Boleyn had been his mistress. Whether this be true or not, it is difficult to say; but it is certain that Thomas Wyatt admitted that he had committed some kind of moral offence, for reference to it is made in the letters of his father, Sir Henry Wyatt, to Cromwell and to the king. The chronicler correctly states that Wyatt was immediately restored to royal favour, and that he was shortly afterwards sent as ambassador to Spain.

Appendix 2

Grounds for the Divorce of Anne

Dr Lingard, in his History of England, expressed the opinion that the marriage between Henry and Anne was decreed by Cranmer to have been null and void from the beginning, because of the former relation of the king to Anne's sister Mary Boleyn. For this he was taken to task by an 'eminent writer'. In the Appendix to the fourth volume of his History he replied to his critic; and every impartial reader will, I think, be convinced by his able and temperate answer. Mr Froude, however, rejects the theory, repeating some of the old arguments of Dr Lingard's opponent, and adding others which he considers very important.

It may be well, therefore, to re-state briefly the whole case. I have already given my reasons for believing that Mary Boleyn had been the mistress of Henry VIII; but I fully agree with Mr Froude that the two questions are to a certain extent independent of one another, and that, even if Mary Boleyn had been Henry's mistress, the divorce may have been granted by Cranmer on different grounds.

The first of Mr Froude's arguments is that in the statute by which Elizabeth was disinherited there occurs in the preamble the following passage:

> ... certain just true and lawful impediment unknown at the making of the said Acts and since that time confessed by the said Lady Anne before the most reverend father in God, Thomas, archbishop

of Canterbury, Metropolitan and Primate of all England, sitting
judicially for the same by the which plainly appeareth ...

In answer to this it may be said, first of all, that if preambles to Acts
of Parliament were to be accepted as trustworthy evidence as to the
facts they recite, English history would be a very strange tale – even
stranger than it appears in Mr Froude's pages. Again, the Act sets
forth that Anne confessed an impediment before Cranmer 'sitting
judicially for the same'. Now, when Cranmer sat at Lambeth on 17
May, Anne was represented by Dr Wotton and Dr Barbour; and, as Dr
Lingard urged some forty years ago, any confession which she may be
said to have made must have been made in her name by her proctors.
Mr Froude evidently feels that there is some force in this argument,
for to strengthen his case he says of Anne that: 'On Wednesday she
was taken to Lambeth, where she made her confession in form, and
the Archbishop, sitting judicially, pronounced her marriage with the
king to have been null and void.' But Mr Froude adduces no evidence
for this remarkable statement. It is most unlikely that if Anne had
been taken from the Tower to Lambeth and back, no reference would
have been made to the fact by chroniclers and newsletter writers, by
Kingston, and by Chapuis. The official record of the court held by
Cranmer expressly excludes the possibility of her having appeared
before him at that time. All the persons who were present are
enumerated, and her name is not in the list. It is stated that she was
represented by N. Wotton and J. Barbour, and the words *personaliter
comparens*, which are always found in such records when the party
chiefly concerned was in court, are wanting. No weight, therefore,
can be attached to Mr Froude's argument, unless he can show that
Cranmer held two different courts for the same purpose, that Anne
was really taken to Lambeth to appear at one of them, and that her
marriage was twice annulled by the archbishop.

In *Chronicle of England under the Tudors*, written apparently by
some cousin of Thomas Wriothesley, who became Lord Chancellor
and Earl of Southampton, occurs the following passage:

And the same day in the afternoon at a solemn court kept at Lambeth
by the Lord Archbishop of Canterbury and the doctors of the law, the
king was divorced from his wife, Queen Anne, and there at the same

court was a privy contract approved that she had made to the Earl of Northumberland afore the king's time, and so she was discharged and was never lawful Queen of England, and there it was approved the same.

Mr Froude accepts this as sound evidence; but he does not say that the only copy of the manuscript of the Chronicle known to exist is certainly later than the year 1592. Though it is pretty certain that the original Chronicle was written by a contemporary, all we have of it is a copy made at a much later date by a scribe who can be proved to have taken considerable liberties with the text. It is, therefore, impossible to decide how much of the manuscript is the work of the author, and how much is due to interpolations and alterations by the copyist.

This fact detracts considerably from the authority of the Chronicle. The phrase about the divorce stands quite apart from the statement that a pre-contract was proved, and the latter explanatory sentence may well have been an interpolation.

But even admitting for argument's sake that the passage was written by the chronicler himself, it cannot be regarded as an important contribution to the discussion of the question. The writer was certainly not a man of high station who had access to the very best information. At the time when his chronicle seems to have been written, his cousin, Thomas Wriothesley, had not risen to eminence, and Sir Thomas Audeley, who appears to have been his patron, was wise enough not to tell the secrets of the king. The chronicler, therefore, had no special knowledge as to secret events; and even about matters regarding which he might have been expected to have accurate information he falls into some very palpable mistakes. He asserts that Henry and Jane Seymour were secretly married at Chelsea, while all other evidence tends to show that the ceremony was performed at Hampton Court. And in the passage quoted by Mr Froude there are also some very grave errors as to fact. For the chronicler says that the court was held on the afternoon of 17 May, while it appears from the official record that it was held between nine and eleven o'clock in the morning. He says, moreover, that Cranmer sat with the doctors of the law, while Cranmer, according to the same official account, sat alone. A writer who makes two such mistakes is certainly not a very trustworthy authority, and his assertion, if it be his, is not to be taken as of equal weight with that of Chapuis.

It is true that Mr Froude tries to discredit the account of Chapuis by asserting that he had at first offered two explanations of the divorce. But in the despatches of Chapuis I have not found these two explanations. The ambassador did say in a letter to Granvelle that he had heard from some people that Cranmer had declared Elizabeth to be the daughter of Noreys, and not of the king, while, according to others, Cranmer had decreed that the marriage between Henry and Anne was invalid on account of the king's former cohabitation with Mary Boleyn. I think it is only Mr Froude who will call this two explanations of the divorce. Chapuis, in June, simply confirmed his first statement as to the grounds of Cranmer's sentence.

A further reason for disbelieving the account of the chronicler and the theory of Mr Froude is that, if the marriage had been pronounced void on account of a pre-contract, this would have had some consequences of which we do not find any trace. First of all, it would have prevented Elizabeth from being declared a bastard, for the good faith of even one of the parents was sufficient to legitimate the issue. As Henry could not well have said that when he married Anne he knew there was a pre-contract with Northumberland, he would necessarily have been held to have acted in good faith. Secondly, the same pre-contract which would have annulled the marriage of Anne and Henry would have annulled that of Lord and Lady Northumberland. We know that the countess wished to be separated from the earl; she would certainly, therefore, have asked for a divorce if it could have been obtained. There is not the slightest evidence that she even thought of making such an application after Anne's death.

If all these arguments be added to those adduced by Dr Lingard, it cannot be seriously doubted that the cause of nullity which Henry was afraid to avow, was his former connection with Mary Boleyn.